MATCHING YOUR MESSAGE TO THE AUDIENCE

A Practical Guide to Structuring Language for New Administrators

Robert A. Pauker and K. Michael Hibbard

Published in partnership with the
American Association of School Administrators

ROWMAN & LITTLEFIELD EDUCATION

A division of
ROWMAN & LITTLEFIELD PUBLISHERS, INC.
Lanham • New York • Toronto • Plymouth, UK

Case studies and scenarios given in this book do not reflect the behaviors or actions of any specific individual.

Published in partnership with the
American Association of School Administrators

Published by Rowman & Littlefield Education
A division of Rowman & Littlefield Publishers, Inc.
A wholly owned subsidiary of
The Rowman & Littlefield Publishing Group, Inc.
4501 Forbes Boulevard, Suite 200, Lanham, Maryland 20706
www.rowman.com

10 Thornbury Road, Plymouth PL6 7PP, United Kingdom

Copyright © 2013 by Robert A. Pauker and K. Michael Hibbard

All rights reserved. No part of this book may be reproduced in any form or by any electronic or mechanical means, including information storage and retrieval systems, without written permission from the publisher, except by a reviewer who may quote passages in a review.

British Library Cataloguing in Publication Information Available

Library of Congress Cataloging-in-Publication Data Available

ISBN 978-1-4758-0391-4 (cloth)—978-1-4758-0392-1 (pbk.)
ISBN 978-1-4758-0393-8 (ebook)

To my brother, whose constant search for knowledge is an inspiration to me, and to my sons, who inspire me to be a better individual.

—Robert Pauker

To my mother, who taught me that "it is what you say and the way you say it!"

—Mike Hibbard

Contents

Preface vii

PART I: UNDERSTANDING THE AUDIENCE OF THE MESSAGE

1 Creating a Communication Match 3
2 Choosing the Right Language 21
3 Thinking More about the Message Recipient 31
4 Applying What You Have Learned 43

PART II: USING THE STRUCTURAL PYRAMID TO GET YOUR POINT ACROSS

5 Using the Subject as the Filter of Your Message 53
6 Making the Verb the Engine of Your Message 75
7 Organizing Your Message with the Proper Perspective 97
8 Deciding Which Part of Your Statement to Emphasize 115

Bibliography 133
About the Authors 135

Preface

Both of us have spent countless hours working in elementary, middle, and high schools. We recognize that success depends on a well-functioning communications system within each of these buildings. Yet too often the words exchanged between administrators and staff members create tension and fail to promote a safe and comfortable learning environment.

This book has been designed to address this issue.

Administrators make decisions to communicate in order to encourage staff members to develop more professional responsibility in school. Administrators should not feel that they have to solve every problem themselves, nor should they always want to transfer the entire weight of a problem or issue to someone else. A prime goal of communication is to encourage staff to be active thinkers who are involved in solving problems and making decisions that improve the school. The school administrator needs to structure communication so it creates a bridge that encourages staff members to become these active thinkers.

We also recognize that the building administrator of today is responsible for a barrage of changes that are initiated at the federal, state, and local levels. These demands are in addition to the administrator's own recognition of changes necessary for success with the school. Therefore, time is of the essence. The paradigm presented in our book can increase the efficiency of organizing both spoken and written communication. All it will take is a little practice on your part.

How does the building administrator communicate with staff members so that they appreciate the significance of the spoken or written message? In essence, the administrator must construct key messages so that the audience is open to receiving the information. Sometimes your audience already accepts the main ideas you are presenting. However, at other times this is not the case. Without doubt, there are many circumstances that affect whether a staff member is open to accepting your point of view, or at least open to considering your perspective. This book is designed to provide a set of principles and strategies that heighten the likelihood of a positive response from the listener or reader of your message.

Of course, people are different. Some are more flexible, while others are more rigid. Some individuals are interested in fostering the common good, while other are more focused on themselves. Most staff members are clearly professional, but a select number of them are less so. Given that the building administrator must implement policy to a wide range of people, we wanted to provide guidelines for communicating the same message to individuals who don't possess similar degrees of flexibility, group concern, or professionalism.

We have observed how one misplaced word or phrase can result in a negative reaction to an important message. People are sensitive to the way language is structured, and they are sensitive to a choice of wording that establishes a tone. Our goal has been to provide a set of techniques for structuring sentences and paragraphs that will increase the probability of a positive reader or listener response.

This book is divided into two parts. The first centers on the key concept of matching how you communicate with the receptivity of the audience. The second part focuses on how to structure sentences and paragraphs in order to receive a maximized response. Each part contains strategies and principles for matching optimum language to the nature of the audience.

Analytical exercises to improve your understanding are imbedded in the text; these have been designed to help you implement these strategies and principles more easily and more effectively. We are excited to share our thoughts and ideas with you.

Robert A. Pauker
Ridgefield, Connecticut

K. Michael Hibbard
North Salem, New York

Part I

UNDERSTANDING THE AUDIENCE OF THE MESSAGE

1
Creating a Communication Match

Introduction

As a school administrator, you are constantly faced with opportunities to communicate with staff. Some of these opportunities call for expedient responses or points of information. Others require serious forethought because the message will have an impact on the success of your school. With each of these opportunities, the choices you make regarding structure, language, and tone will have an impact on the attitude of the message recipient. Making the best choices often will determine whether the reader or listener readily accepts your point of view.

Even though the pressures of time often require a quickly produced message, school administrators need to consider options for structuring language in a meaningful way. By matching the message to the listener, the administrator increases the likelihood that the content of the message will be received clearly. In essence, this matching process tends to eliminate both external and internal baggage that may prevent the listener or reader from receiving the message openly.

The goal of the administrator communicating information is to sell his or her message to the audience, whether the recipient is an individual or a group. Casually presenting a key policy or concept can be risky. Planning the optimum structure of the message creates a greater likelihood of support. By effectively structuring spoken or written sentences, the administrator can create a positive atmosphere. This positive feeling results in a heightened openness to the main ideas presented.

School administrators communicate formally with parents, teachers, members of the community, and other administrators within their school district. In each of these instances, the administrator needs to be conscious of selling his or her message to the listener or reader. Regardless of the recipient, the speaker or writer needs to keep certain significant questions at the forefront of his or her thinking.

- What is my prior experience with this person or group?
- How will this prior experience influence message receptivity?
- What are the definable traits of the message recipient that will affect getting my point across?
- What is the actual purpose of my message?
- How am I trying to change behavior through this message?

The principal needs to train his or her mind to center on key questions that will affect the message. Thinking about how to structure the message around responses to these questions will have a major impact on the willingness of the listener or reader to accept the content of the message.

In essence, the principal benefits from engaging in a thinking process to be used prior to writing or speaking important messages. This process considers three key components that interact with each other.

- First, the administrator determines the desired *behavior* of the person receiving the message.
- Second, the administrator considers the nature of the *person* or group receiving the message.
- Third, the administrator thinks about how he or she can use the physical and social *environment* to sell the message to others.

In the technologically oriented society of today, most people do not reflect on the best way to structure their message. People are caught up in a constant mind-set of speed. As people "twitter" and e-mail, their goal is often to finish the message without thinking about its recipient. One clear benefit of applying reflection to the structure and delivery of the message is that the writer or speaker can have a positive influence over the attitude of the listener or reader. When this occurs, the listener or reader tends to have a heightened comprehension of the message content.

Thinking about the Audience

As a school administrator, you have the responsibility to communicate clearly and coherently with staff. Too often administrators assume this responsibility without considering the optimum ways of getting their point across. The message is either too directive or too nebulous. Communication, either spoken or written, is enhanced when the speaker or writer considers this important question: Who is the person or people with whom I am communicating?

By "people" in this question, we don't just mean a group, such as fourth grade teachers. In this instance, "people" also refers to the observable personality traits of those receiving the message.

For the school administrator about to speak or write with some or all of his or her staff, the concept of personality and communication relates to three key factors. These are flexibility, friendship, and professionalism. These three factors were initially presented by psychologists O. J. Harvey, David E. Hunt, and Harold M. Schroder in their famous work *Conceptual Systems and Personality Organization*.

Here are some scenarios designed to explain each of the three factors.

- Flexibility—Fred is tolerant of new ideas and always willing to try out strategies and materials. Fred's principal has

asked him to pilot a new science program. Realizing that the current program is deficient, Fred agrees after reviewing the material favorably.
- Friendship—Juanita values the importance of collegiality and is sensitive, respectful, and open to the opinions and comments of her peers. The principal has asked Juanita to create a draft for new lesson planning forms. She works with her colleagues to create and get feedback on the draft. The final product reflects the consensus of the group.

The person who values people (friendship) is empathetic and flexible to the needs of others, while the person who does not value people tends to be more hostile and aggressive. The administrator should try to recognize which staff members value people since these individuals will value the opinions of others, listen, and learn from others on their own.

- Professionalism—Carl is respectful of others, knowledgeable, well prepared for instruction, and has appropriate relationships with students and adults. The principal has asked Carl to be on a committee to improve student performance in mathematics across grade levels. Carl solicits ideas from other teachers and parents. He reviews the research and finds that improving assessments and using data to make instructional decisions is highly correlated with improving student performance. He works with his committee to create, implement, and assess new strategies.

The person who is professional tends to display certain pedagogical characteristics, such as understanding content, designing well-crafted lessons, and analyzing student strengths and weakness.

Harvey, Hunt, and Schroder define four types of conceptual development of individuals. The first type of individual displays *unilateral dependence*. This is an individual who relies on external control; he or she seeks the approval and direction of others. The second type of individual they define shows *negative indepen-*

dence. This individual tends to be hostile or aggressive by nature. The third type has *conditional dependence and mutuality*. This is someone who will listen to alternative points of view, is more adapting and accepting, and is more objective. The fourth type of individual is characterized by *interdependence*. This fourth-stage individual can openly explore options, is highly flexible to changing conditions, and is autonomous by nature.

Effective communication depends on the principal's understanding of each of these four types. However, the administrator can more easily boil down his or her thinking to one key word—*flexibility*. If the message recipient is flexible, then, regardless of all other attitudes and beliefs, he or she will be more likely to listen to the meaning of the message before reacting.

The highly flexible person is able to adapt to changing conditions and is very willing to explore options that will solve problems. The individual who is less flexible either tends to seek external control—meaning the approval of others—or tends to be hostile toward authority. The implications for communicating with someone at either end of the spectrum are enormous. The flexible person wants change if change will improve the quality of the learning environment. The hostile or aggressive person does not trust change; this individual might resent the principal's authority. The message recipient who is flexible needs to be treated differently from the less flexible individual.

Of course, the principal is not going to determine levels of flexibility with absolute accuracy. The point is for the principal to consider how flexible an individual has been in the past. Does the message recipient tend to be a problem solver? Is the recipient willing to entertain options?

In addition, the administrator needs to remember that the message recipient who is dependent upon the approval of others is going to wait until others respond to the message before stating a response. The person who tends to be hostile toward the principal is going to criticize the message regardless of its content. The group of teachers who are more flexible can make up their own minds, but, most importantly, they are very interested in what is best for the larger group. The staff members who are flexible form a great problem-solving team.

These factors of flexibility are an easy way for the administrator to think about the individuals with whom he or she interacts. In summary, here are a few ideas to keep in mind.

- Less flexible people do not want to change, even when circumstances dictate the need for a change.
- The person who is not flexible because he or she cannot think for him- or herself is associated with stage one. The school administrator needs to communicate with a less flexible person differently than with a highly flexible person.
- The flexible individual recognizes alternative points of view and is open to exploring options.
- The person who is not flexible tends to like things the way they are or long for conditions that existed in the past.
- The person who is highly flexible tends to embrace changing conditions, as long as these new conditions are perceived as beneficial to the larger learning environment.

Finally, the school administrator needs to keep in mind that this type of thinking is not designed to construct a complete psychological profile of any individual or group. The goal is to gain valuable insights based on observable behavior. A person who resents change in the past requires a different approach than a person who has embraced change in the past.

It is also essential to keep in mind that many teachers are highly competent even though they may not be flexible in nature. These individuals are often valuable members of staff who require a step-by-step sequence of communication in order to convince them that an idea is worth implementing. This is directly parallel to the concept of varying an instructional approach for certain students; the goal for learning is the same, but the approach is different.

Here is the bottom line. The effectiveness of an administrator's communication depends on understanding the characteristics of the audience. If the audience is flexible, values the experiences of colleagues, and is professional, the structure of the message needs to be different than if each of these characteristics is low.

The principal needs to know how to communicate with all types of individuals. One message recipient might be highly flexible; another message recipient might be less flexible but still maintain a strong desire to do what is best for the students. The administrator needs to respect both of these individuals. However, the way in which he or she communicates with the first recipient will be different from the approach with the second.

Exercise to Increase Understanding and Promote Discussion

The content of this section focuses on recognizing the flexibility of the message recipient. Select one individual with whom you have worked who would rank at the higher end of the spectrum of flexibility and an individual who would rank low on the spectrum. Do not mention any names. Write a brief profile for each individual related to these traits. You can base your description on anecdotes or specific observations. You can think of several different individuals and create a composite profile.

What makes one person more flexible?

_____
_____
_____
_____

What factor would you need to keep in mind when communicating with the person who is less flexible?

_____
_____
_____
_____

What conclusion can you draw that will help you in future communications?

_____

_____

_____

Thinking about the Message Tone

As an administrator, you are expected to create an environment that is professional, flexible, and friendly. The way you communicate with the members of your staff will determine whether these three factors are present in the day-to-day functioning of your school. It is essential to take a positive approach toward the structure your message.

If the language you use to initiate, inform, and respond to teachers has negative overtones, then your capacity for implementing change and for encouraging personal growth will be minimized. Your communication style can be very demanding and still elicit the types of responses that result in a positive, powerful school environment.

Be aware of the sensitivity of the message recipient. In simple terms, some people are more sensitive to certain messages than others. Your goal is to inform and to persuade, to establish criteria that may or may not be initially accepted. The way in which you communicate these criteria will often change from person to person and from group to group.

This idea is similar to how we expect teachers to work with students. In order to achieve classroom objectives, we expect differentiated instruction. In essence, as an administrator, you must engage in differentiated communication. Matching the tone of the communication to the sensitivity of the person receiving the message will ensure better results.

The tone of every message has implications. As an administrator, you need to think about tonal implications. A tonal implication is how the sound of the message resonates with the listener or reader. Certain types of music are tonally pleasing to you. Other types of music are not. The same is true with words. How the listener or reader hears the message affects his or her feelings at the moment of reception. This either increases or decreases appreciation and a willingness to receive the meaning of the message.

When you are feeling threatened by the surrounding environment, you are less open to hearing the true meaning of the message. If you feel comfortable in the surrounding environment, you are more open to hearing the true meaning of the message. As an administrator, you want to make sure that the "melody" of your words enhances the likelihood that the recipient hears the content as accurately as possible.

Just think about these three basic sentences. After you have read all three, think about the difference in tone for each.

Sentence 1: Sharpen your pencil quickly.
Sentence 2: Please, sharpen your pencil quickly.
Sentence 3: You must sharpen your pencil quickly.

The first sentence is a command; the recipient of the message is ordered to conduct an action. The second sentence is also a command; however, the word *please* removes the dictatorial nature of the order. The final statement is not technically a command; the sentence begins with the subject *you* instead of being implied, as in the other two examples. In addition, the final sentence uses the helping verb *must*, which conveys a requirement.

Each of these three statements is heard differently by the listener. The administrator's role as a speaker or writer is to determine which sentence structure will best allow the recipient to accept the message in a positive manner.

Think about these three sentences from a classroom teacher's point of view. For many students, it does not make any difference which of the three sentence options the teacher would use to communicate the message. However, there are certain students who need to hear the word *please* and other students who need to hear the helping verb *must*. In the classroom, the teacher has a moment to determine which structure will result in the execution of the prescribed behavior.

The same idea is true for the principal. He or she has a moment to determine how the message should be structured. As a principal, you need to keep this idea in mind.

Thinking about Communication Matches

How can the principal become more cognizant of creating better communication matches? As a principal, you can increase communication matches by recognizing the *flexibility, friendship,* and *professionalism* of the individual or group receiving your message. In order to accomplish this result, you need to consider responses to these three basic questions.

> The concept of a "communication match" is based on the premise that *each individual possesses his or her own levels of sensitivity to language*. This sensitivity changes from situation to situation.

Question 1: How flexible is the message recipient, and how flexible do I have to be in the structure of my communication?

You need to consider how flexible this person or particular group has been in the past. If the message recipient views the world in a very cut-and-dried fashion, then you will need to structure you message differently than if this recipient has been flexible in the past.

The key is to think about how the recipient has reacted to change in the past. If you have limited prior experience with the recipient, then try for a middle ground in your communication. Here are two examples of part of a memorandum informing the teacher in charge of social studies about a professional development requirement. The first addresses a flexible recipient, while the second is tailored to a less flexible recipient.

Ms. Jones has volunteered to train all social studies teachers how to use Smart Boards more effectively during instruction. It is important that this training take place during the next month. Contact Ms. Jones to set up an optimum time for this training.

Ms. Jones will be training all social studies teachers in techniques for using Smart Boards more effectively during instruction. This training will begin on Tuesday, November 3, from 3:00 to 4:30 in Ms. Jones's classroom.

The sentences directed to the flexible recipient inform him or her of the requirement but let the logistics be worked out with Ms. Jones. The second set of sentences is much more directive because the principal knows that the teacher in charge or the teachers receiving training will not follow through independently.

If the principal structures sentences for a flexible teacher and, in fact, the teacher is not flexible, the message recipient is less likely to act in the expected manner. In essence, this is considered a mismatch. Here is rule of thumb to keep in mind: A more flexible message recipient will be more likely to respond positively to a message, regardless of the structure. A less flexible message recipient will only respond in the desired manner if the message is more focused in nature.

Question 2: How friendly do I need to make the message?

Friendliness does not refer to socialization. Friendliness refers to the formality implied by the nouns and verbs in the structure of the message. For example, here are two statements that have essentially the same meaning. Which one is more friendly in nature?

I will tell team leaders to work with you in creating a schedule.

I will talk with the team leaders about working with you in developing a schedule.

The verb tends to have the greatest impact in determining the level of friendliness in the message. The verb *tell* is more formal than the verb *talk*.

Even though the difference between the two statements is nominal, the principal needs to be aware of how formally the message recipient needs to be treated. Generally, more flexible individuals tend to have less of a need for formality.

When writing, you will tend to be more formal. However, when speaking, you will need to make instantaneous choices between more formal and less formal nouns and verbs. The reality is that the message recipient's attitude about the message can change drastically if the speaker's choices do not reflect the need for appropriate formality.

Question 3: What aspects of professionalism do I need to keep in mind?

Professionalism can be viewed from many different angles. How well does the teacher understand his or her content? How well does the teacher understand the curriculum? What is the teacher's pedagogy? How prepared is the teacher for class? How well does the teacher relate to students? How open is the teacher to new materials, strategies, or technologies that enhance the quality of instruction? What is the attitude of the teacher toward colleagues?

Each of these questions is part of a list that the administrator needs to consider when structuring the message. The teacher who does not have a strong understanding of content is going to become very defensive about any topic related to instruction. The teacher who insists on instructing his or her way and not applying the demands of the curriculum is going to be resistant. The teacher who has never thought about the art of teaching may require leading by colleagues in order to implement any type of change. The teacher who is not prepared for class needs a different type of structural message than a teacher who is prepared but is lacking in one area. All of these factors influence the way the administrator organizes the message and the language used in it.

Here are two situations to illustrate the point:

Situation One

Mr. S. is a middle school music teacher and department chairperson. He is responsible for organizing and leading an end-of-the-year assembly for the entire student body that features the school's music performing groups. He is feeling a lot of pressure because his rehearsal time has been reduced due to field trips, other assemblies, and state testing. The music teacher has requested a meeting with the school principal, Dr. B., in order to share his frustration and to garner support for extra practice sessions for the chorus and band.

Dr. B. knows that Mr. S. tends to be fair and honest when meeting with administrators. Mr. S. is less flexible by nature but does work hard to present a top-notch concert. He will often times generate "yes, buts" in order to prevent change. In this instance, Mr. S. has faced a change in schedule that has resulted in less rehearsal time. In response, Mr. S. is asking for others to change their schedules so he can have extra rehearsal time.

After thinking about these traits of the teacher and reflecting on the quality of past concerts, the principal instinctively recognizes that she might initiate the same message in three different ways. In this instance, the principal is meeting with the music teacher. Therefore, the message is to be spoken. Each of these initiations will have a different impact on the listener—the message recipient.

Certainly, there are scores of possible options that the principal might consider. However, she also needs to be comfortable with the structure of the sentences. Therefore, the principal quickly thinks about these three options.

> **Option 1:** I want this assembly to be terrific. I value what you and your colleagues do. I want to work with you to solve this problem.

Option 2: Your work is exemplary. The assembly needs to be at the same high quality as last year's. The problem is significant.

Option 3: Everyone wants your music students to succeed in their performance. We all value what you and your colleagues do. The staff and I can work with you to solve the problem.

The first option implies that the principal will help solve the problem. The second option recognizes the problem, but leaves the burden of solution on the back of Mr. S. In the third option, the principal is speaking for the entire staff and is indicating that the staff would be willing to show the flexibility necessary to assist with the solution.

It is essential to remember that the initiation of the message often is the most powerful component in enhancing the receptivity of the message recipient. In this case, the music teacher doubts that the principal is empathetic or flexible; he thinks that all administrators are "top-down" bureaucrats.

The principal needs to match her sentence structure with the likely receptivity of the listener. Does the listener want the administrator to solve the problem? Does the listener want praise but really wants to address the problem him- or herself? Does the listener want to be reassured that the staff supports his efforts?

The three introductory comments by the principal are very similar in meaning. However, the receptive capacity of the listener will be heightened by the best choice. The speaker needs to lower anxiety and send a positive message in order to achieve the goal of a successful concert. Even though this individual is not highly flexible, the principal knows that the music teacher is very professional; previous music concerts have been excellent. In this instance, the principal would likely choose the third option because it is the most disarming to someone who tends to be defensive.

The desired behavioral outcome is for the music chairperson to feel that he is valued by the principal and that the principal will help ensure that the assembly is a success. The principal is structuring her comments for a message recipient who is not highly flexible, does not feel that the staff is friendly enough, but is still highly professional.

Of course, the realities of the situation could be different. The principal might be dealing with a music chairperson who is very different from the individual in the first scenario. This idea leads to the second case study.

Situation Two

Now let's look at a different scenario. Let's suppose that the principal believes the music teacher has frittered away valuable time and has not been very organized in the development of the program. In fact, the principal has been aware that the music teacher has not used available rehearsal time wisely. She has discussed this with the music teacher on two separate occasions. The principal wants the concert to be a success but is not willing to advocate taking extra time from other classes beyond the "pull-out" time already scheduled.

In the previous scenario, the music teacher worked hard and used time wisely. In this situation, the music teacher has not maximized his use of allotted time; as a result, the principal is not pleased. As was communicated above, the principal has spoken with this teacher in the past. The effectiveness of this communication is questionable because there has not been any real change in the music teacher's behavior.

The three options of initiation that the principal considers in this situation are different than in the first scenario. Each option of initial communication will have an impact on whether the music teacher listens to the rest of the message or not. Again, the principal is going to meet with the music teacher; therefore, the message is spoken as opposed to written. The options for introductory comments might be as follows:

> **Option 1:** The assembly is an important part of our year. We have talked about my concern that you have not taken advantage of the rehearsal time allotted. I cannot support taking students out of other classes at this stage of the academic year.

Option 2: You still have some rehearsal time left. Please use it as efficiently as possible so our students will have a good experience.

Option 3: Every member of the staff has a lot on his or her plate. Each teacher is trying to maximize student performance in his or her class for the end of the year. Each teacher needs every allotted minute to achieve this result.

The first option chastises the music teacher. The second option emphasizes that the music teacher only gets the predetermined allotted time; the principal communicates that it is the music teacher's responsibility to use the time wisely. The principal is not owning the responsibility. The third option represents the principal speaking for the rest of the staff. Even though the nature of each message is very similar, the innuendo connected with that message is very different.

Every message poses an attitude. The receiver of the message absorbs that attitude. This initial response colors the way the rest of the message is received. No two people receive the same spoken message identically. Therefore, the degrees of perceived flexibility, friendliness, and professionalism contained in a message are based on the personality of the recipient.

For example, one music teacher might view option three on the previous page as an insult, while another music teacher might view the comment as logical. In both cases, the principal perceives that the music teacher is trying to divert the responsibility. Therefore, the administrator avoids this mistake by not agreeing to accept responsibility for the problem. Each of the three options is based on the premise that the music teacher must accept the responsibility. The principal must decide which of the three options best achieves this goal. Without doubt, the way the message is received will impact how the listener responds.

Always remember . . .
You need to select the language option that will most likely result in the desired behavior.

Exercises to Increase Understanding and Promote Discussion

Pretend you are the music teacher described in situation two below. Which of the three options of the principal would have the most favorable tonal implication for you? Tell why you made this choice.

_____
_____
_____

Tell which of the options would have the least favorable tonal implication for you and discuss why.

_____
_____
_____

Personal experience has an impact on tonal implication. There is no way, as an administrator, that you can fully understand an individual's situation outside of your school. However, it is important to be sensitive to the idea of past experience if some level of knowledge exists. For example, if a teacher is going through a divorce, and you know this is difficult for him or her, there may be a heightened sensitivity to the idea of being told what to do by a member of the opposite sex. This does not mean that you should refrain from communicating significant issues, but it does mean that *how* you discuss them might need an added level of sensitivity.

Think of an experience in your life that has had an effect on how you heard the messages of others. For example, this experience might relate to a parent who was always telling you what to do.

_____
_____
_____

Think of a time when you had to adjust the structure of what you said or wrote because the person with whom you were communicating was facing a difficult personal experience. How did you adjust your message so that it was clear but more sensitive?

_____

_____

Now, think of another situation where you had to consider two options for structuring the message to an individual. Record both options below. Before you write, consider these three factors about the individual:

Flexibility of the individual: _____

_____

Friendship of the individual: _____

_____

Professionalism of the individual: _____

_____

Message option 1: _____

     _____

     _____

     _____

     _____

     _____

Message option 2: _____

     _____

     _____

     _____

     _____

2
Choosing the Right Language

Using Language to Think about the Recipient

Language can become an administrator's greatest selling tool. It can be used for inspiration or to inhibit action. By recognizing the options available in structuring language, the administrator can determine how to maximize a positive attitude in the recipient. In some people's minds, this concept represents manipulation with a questionable purpose. However, consider the following:

- The president of the United States employs a speechwriting team in order to maximize the public's positive response to issues.
- Successful doctors vary their approaches to consultations depending on perceived anxieties of patients.
- A successful auto mechanic will speak differently to a customer with a technical background than to a customer with little understanding of cars.

Each of these situations is a purposeful manipulation of language in order to convince the listener of the significance of information. However, this type of language manipulation presents information in an honest and accurate way for the purpose of communicating clearly with a specific audience. The goal is for the receiver of the information to comprehend the message clearly. The presenter of the message wants the receiver to respond in an appropriate way. This idea is true in many professions.

When a doctor manipulates the way information is presented in order to reduce anxiety in a particular patient, this manipulation will include content, word choice, sentence structure, tone, and body language *but never data and appropriate steps for treatment*. The level of anxiety is different for each patient. If the doctor is familiar with the personality and history of his or her patients, he or she will create different ways of sharing the same messages. As a result, patient anxiety can be reduced while still communicating essential information.

A significant underlying question for optimized written and spoken communication is this: How does the administrator quickly determine the design of meaningful language options?

Kurt Lewin, the revered psychologist, maintained the following: behavior is a function of person interacting with environment. Thirty years after Lewin expounded this idea, David Hunt, another famous psychologist, used Lewin's paradigm as the basis of his book *Between Psychology and Education*. In this book, Dr. Hunt creates several situations in which teachers, administrators, and counselors figure out how to change the school environment given this premise.

It is impossible to change the personality (or person). The best way to change behavior, according to Hunt, is to alter the physical or social environment. By doing this, a student's personality will interact with a different environment, thereby producing a new (hopefully more acceptable or productive) behavior.

This same concept applies to you as an administrator in communicating effectively to a variety of individuals and groups. You are *not* going to change anyone's basic *person*. You can get your message across better by asking this: How can I use language and create the best physical and social environment to increase the recipient's comfort with my message?

The bottom line is to match language and the environment to the immediate situation. This matching process happens by keeping certain factors in mind, including the following:

- Using the right sentence subjects
- Employing the optimum verb
- Communicating in a comfortable location
- Determining the type of message

Always remember . . .
If you want to change the behavior of a person, then you must be aware of key traits that will help or hinder the recipient's acceptance of your message.

Applying This Understanding to the Classroom

This same idea is identical to the manner in which a teacher and administrator approach a problem student. For example, if a student in a high school class has not taken an assignment seriously and is constantly talking to other students during class, the teacher might contact the vice principal out of desperation. The teacher would expect some type of intervention from the vice principal that would result in two obvious changes in that student's behavior. First, the student would stop distracting other students. Second, the student would work seriously on class assignments and complete them after the teacher has appropriately modified his or her presentation of the material.

In this situation, the vice principal is going to find out necessary background information about current student and teacher behavior. The vice principal would study the student's school records and observe the student in class as well as in other school settings. He or she would then determine characteristics that define who this student is. This type of information about the student could look like this:

- Does not perform well in the class
- Seeks attention through minor, irritating behaviors such as talking to other students
- Performs above average on state tests

24 / Chapter 2

- Is successful as an athlete on a team with a demanding coach
- Has parents who are not involved in school

This information would enable the vice principal to think about the student's strengths and weaknesses. Of note is that the student does not focus in class but can focus on the playing field. In addition, the vice principal notes that the student performs poorly in class but well on state tests. These differences enlighten the vice principal to the possible potential of the student. The vice principal then studies the teacher's performance reviews and observes the teacher interacting with that student. The administrator might arrive at these types of conclusions about the *person* of the teacher.

- Tends to be rigid and does not differentiate instruction
- Tends to be an information presenter and does not actively involve students in learning
- Tends to be intolerant of students who do not "cooperate" in class
- Students who "cooperate" are successful

By thinking about the person of the teacher, the vice principal recognizes immediately the potential mismatch between the student and the teacher. To solve the problem, the vice principal needs to communicate with both the student and the teacher. However, he or she will have to construct two different messages. In constructing these two messages, the vice principal will need to consider content, word choice, sentence structure, tone, and body language. The nature of each message must be based

> **You must keep this in mind . . .**
> The administrator's observations need to be realistic. This idea is essential for teachers and students. Comments need to be based on observation and data. At times, it will be tempting to place personal feeling about a person ahead of valid commentary. This is unacceptable.

on traits of the student and the teacher. The vice principal determines the types of environmental change that will be necessary to accomplish the desired behaviors of the student and of the teacher in order for change to occur.

In this illustration, the administrator's observations reveal the mismatch between the teacher and the student. By thinking about the *person* of the teacher, the vice principal recognizes immediately the potential mismatch.

Using the Administrator's Analysis to Maximize Communication

The goal of communication is to create a predicted response (behavior). This predicted response can take many forms. The recipient of the message might be called into action, be asked to solve a problem, need to become a more careful observer, or need to raise key questions. In all cases, the administrator needs to understand the expected behavior based upon the message.

Think back to the example of the music teacher from chapter 1. If the principal wants a positive response from the teacher, he or she will quickly create a set of possible approaches. In the illustration, Dr. G. created three options in her mind to initiate discussion. She needed to select the option that best matches the beliefs and attitudes of the individual. In addition, Dr. G. had to keep in mind her prior relationship with the teacher.

You can begin to ascertain the best language match by asking these types of questions:

- **How independent is this person?** This question helps to determine if the individual can act alone. The recipient of the message may or may not need validation, or the recipient may resent authority.
- **How well do I know this person?** A prior relationship obviously matters. If the administrator is friendly with the recipient, the message may not change, but the structure of the message might.

- **What is my attitude toward the person's concern?** If the administrator feels positive about the concern, then a level of empathy already exists.

In addition to these three questions, the administrator needs to evaluate each of these factors already discussed in chapter 1:

- **How flexible do I need to be?** The level of flexibility built into the initial comments makes a huge difference. If the administrator is dealing with someone who is controlling by nature, he or she needs to indicate a different level of flexibility than if the recipient of the message is independent by nature.
- **How friendly do I need to be in the structure of the message?** Friendliness does not refer to socialization. Friendliness is about the formality implied in the nouns and verbs that structure the message.
- **How professional do I need to be in the structure of the message?** The principal is always professional. However, the level of professionalism as a speaker is determined by the location of the speaker and recipient, as well as the body language of the speaker. For example, in a more formal setting, the speaker might be across from the recipient. Often there will be a desk or table separating them.

The spoken words of the administrator establish the attitudinal environment. In essence, these words establish the connection between what has or is taking place and what will need to take place. Sometimes these differences are significant, and sometimes the differences are minor.

The listener's response is significantly influenced by the structure of the message, and the listener's response is partially determined by his or her personality.

If we think back about the first music teacher example, it is possible to think about the interaction through the chart that follows. This chart is based on the work of David Hunt. In this instance, the music teacher has worked hard and is very competent.

What are the *behaviors* the principal is looking for (what the principal wants to happen)?	Who is this *person* (what this person is like as an individual)?	As a result, what are the *tone* and *structure* of the message (how the principal needs to structure the message in order to create the best result)?
The principal wants to show that the teacher is valued by her and the rest of the faculty. The principal wants to assist the teacher in finding a solution to the problem. The principal wants the teacher to develop more confidence when interacting with the faculty.	The teacher seems to need the approval of others. The teacher is excellent at carrying out policy but is uncomfortable trying to arrive at solutions to any problems that have an impact on instructional success. However, the teacher does tend to recognize problems that arise.	The message from the principal needs to focus on the following: (1) a supportive tone that shows a strong appreciation for hard work; (2) words that shows the principal will help to solve the problem; (3) a request that the teacher create a possible solution to the problem so that the problem is not reoccurring.

This chart shows the principal's determination of how to construct the necessary message. The principal reflects on previous behaviors and attitudes of the teacher. The teacher is not a controlling person, even if he is not highly flexible; he is someone who takes his job seriously and is very competent. The music teacher needs affirmation that the staff will support him. The principal wants to establish a tone that will give the teacher a supportive push.

The other scenario presented earlier painted a picture of a music teacher who was not as professional. The message to this teacher needs to be quite different. The next chart presents an analysis of this second music teacher. The middle and right columns of this chart are very different from those in the previous chart.

What are the *behaviors* the principal is looking for (what the principal wants to happen)?	Who is this *person* (what this person is like as an individual)?	As a result, what are the *tone* and *structure* of the message (how the principal needs to structure the message in order to create the best result)?
The principal wants the teacher to feel responsible for not using time wisely. The principal is not going to provide much assistance. The principal will indicate the poor professionalism of the teacher in end-of-year evaluations.	The teacher expects others to rescue him. The teacher does not pay attention to advice given previously by the principal. The teacher tends to blame others for a below-par showing, including the students. The teacher does not put forth the thinking and planning necessary for the concert.	The message from the principal needs to focus on the following: (1) a tone that reinforces clear expectation of a strong concert; (2) a message that states advice has been given in the past; (3) a structure that uses powerful verbs and an emphasis on the subject pronoun *you*.

Choosing the Right Language / 29

Here is the point: as a principal, you can benefit from using this chart format and recording information and data that will assist you in the structure and tone of your message. Remember, if you practice this format, over time you will automatically think in this logical manner. The chart will be inside your head.

What are the *behaviors* the principal is looking for (what the principal wants to happen)?	Who is this *person* (what this person is like as an individual)?	As a result, what are the *tone* and *structure* of the message (how the principal needs to structure the message in order to create the best result)?
In this column, list the outcome behaviors you would like to occur.	*In this column, list what you know to be true about the individual or group who will receive the message. Avoid personal feelings. Avoid any hearsay. Make sure you consider flexibility, friendliness, and professionalism.*	*In this column, record notes about the structure and tone of the message. Think about the best subjects and verbs. Keep in mind the recipient's flexibility, friendliness, and professionalism.*

3

Thinking More about the Message Recipient

Applying What We Have Learned to a New Case Study

Mr. A. is a social studies teacher in a city high school. He has been in the classroom for twenty-two years. He has traditionally been left alone to prepare his course as he sees fit. He treasures this independence and has in the past bad-mouthed an administrator who tried to alter the content of his courses and the manner in which he presents ideas. The demographics of the students in Mr. A.'s classes are similar to the sections instructed by other teachers. Student performance in his class on the departmental midterm and final exams, as well as on the related state social studies test, has been below that of students in sections taught by other teachers.

A new administrator, Mrs. Y., has arrived at this high school. The central office has made it clear to the new principal that the teaching methodologies of certain "less effective" teachers must change. Mr. A. is on the list. As a new principal, Mrs. Y. decided to spend time observing several classes in the school, including Mr. A.'s. She made sure that "quick visits" were not against the teachers' contract.

While observing Mr. A.'s classes, the new principal drew five conclusions based on her informal data.

1. Mr. A. believes he is a terrific teacher.
2. Mr. A. is organized, but the material being presented is not challenging to students.
3. The students are required to complete simple tasks, such as fill-in-the-blank tests, but are not engaged in higher-level thinking exercises.
4. The material delivered by Mr. A. does not match the prescribed curriculum.
5. Weekly tests or quizzes are not closely matched with the content or structure of the departmental and state assessments.

In addition to spending time in the classroom with students, Mrs. Y. visited Mr. A. during his preparation period in order to learn more about his teaching philosophy. These short discussions revealed that the social studies teacher does not believe students can handle the conceptual difficulty of the prescribed curriculum. Therefore, he is delivering an alternative, "watered-down" curriculum. Mrs. Y. decided to intervene.

She first thought about Mr. A., the person. She ascertained that he does not want to be challenged. He is resistant to change. He believes he is maximizing student learning. He believes that each student has an inherent "ability" and cannot succeed in higher-order learning tasks. He does not believe in encouraging students to improve their intellect (because he believes "intellect" is a fixed trait). The principal decided to spend a few minutes completing the three-column communication analysis chart. She completed the middle column of the chart first.

What are the *behaviors* the principal is looking for (what the principal wants to happen)?	Who is this *person* (what this person is like as an individual)?	As a result, what are the *tone* and *structure* of the message (how the principal needs to structure the message in order to create the best result)?
	What the principal knows to be true about the individual or group who will receive the message. He does not want to challenge himself or his students. He is resistant to change. He thinks he is maximizing learning. He does not encourage students to push their thinking. He is defensive if challenged. He is not very flexible.	

In short, Mrs. Y. realizes that she has to break through a wall in order to achieve change. In addition, Mrs. Y. knows that this teacher is not flexible. She knows that he displays a friendliness to other teachers who agree with him. In addition, Mrs. Y. recognizes that Mr. A.'s professionalism is limited. The principal's next step is to think about the desired outcomes of the message.

What are the *behaviors* the principal is looking for (what the principal wants to happen)?	Who is this *person* (what this person is like as an individual)?	As a result, what are the *tone* and *structure* of the message (how the principal needs to structure the message in order to create the best result)?
The outcome behaviors the principal would like to occur. **Mr. A. teaches using analysis and technology; he eliminates copying notes. He uses higher-quality assignments. He incorporates higher-level thinking into lessons. He works to become better at helping students understand content and differentiating. The teacher records these as goals in his self-improvement plan.**	*What the principal knows to be true about the individual or group who will receive the message.* He does not want to challenge himself or his students. He is resistant to change. He thinks he is maximizing learning. He does not encourage students to push their thinking. He is defensive if challenged. He is not very flexible.	

Mrs. Y. could have listed ten or more ideas in the left column. However, she restricted the listing of outcomes to a manageable number. As principal, you need to adjust the wording of the message so that it becomes more acceptable to the recipient. In this instance, Mrs. Y. has to figure out how to adjust her message to have the greatest impact on Mr. A., the message recipient.

This adjustment can keep the recipient from becoming defensive and resistant to any type of change. In this illustration, the principal knows that Mr. A. has exhibited defensive reactions to previous attempts by administration to push change. Therefore, she must incorporate prior experience into the structure of her message.

Learning about the Right Approach

The principal needs to be aware of options in creating the *best* message structure. Sometimes this kind of adjustment requires altering the focus of the message. In the case of Mr. A., the principal has to decide if the best approach to the message is *direct* or *indirect*.

> A **direct approach** focuses the filter of the message directly at the person or group that needs to change.

> An **indirect approach** focuses on selling the change through a beneficiary of the change.

Mr. A. would become quickly defensive if the principal made a direct statement about changing a specific instructional behavior. However, if the message were stated in terms of student performance—an indirect connection to the teacher's instruction—Mr. A. might be much more accepting. Here are two possible statements Mrs. Y could share with Mr. A.

Direct Approach	*Indirect Approach*
Mr. A., you need to reduce the amount of copying during class presentations and give students the opportunity to analyze important concepts and information—like they are required to do on the state tests.	The students need to improve their higher-order thinking in written responses. These responses need go beyond factual knowledge from their notes to be analytical in nature—like items required on state exams.

Here is an analysis of the principal's thinking on whether to employ a direct or an indirect approach. The principal thinks about the differences between the two types of statements.

The Principal Chooses an Indirect Approach to the Message

In order to achieve the desired instructional changes, Mrs. Y. determined that she had to present them as student changes. The teacher would be far too defensive toward altering his instruction if he believed he was the problem.

The principal's goal was to change Mr. A.'s behavior of spending too much class time having students copy information from the text and to challenge him to spend more time engaging students in higher-order thinking through their speaking and writing. She thought about how to state a student behavior that would push the teacher to undergo an instructional behavioral change. Mrs. Y. arrived at the following: Requiring students to take notes and use them to answer higher-order thinking questions would force Mr. A. to state more meaningful ideas and information during his class presentations. In addition, students would have to be more attentive to what he said because the notes would become required.

The principal has followed a series of steps to help clarify the best possible structure of the message being delivered to this teacher. Here is a review of these steps:

1. The principal thought about the problem or issue.
2. The principal observed the current behaviors of the message recipient (in this case the teacher).
3. The principal thought about the flexibility and professionalism of the message recipient (which were recorded in the middle column of the chart).
4. The principal determined achievable desired outcomes (which were recorded in the left column of the chart).
5. The principal thought about whether to employ a direct or an indirect message style, determining that an indirect approach would be more effective.

Now the principal clarifies and further specifies outcome behaviors.

The Principal's Thinking about the First Behavioral Change

Mrs. Y realized that during Mr. A.'s instruction students were not paying attention. This lack of focus was probably due to boredom. However, the students were not required to do any task except copy off of the board while Mr. A. talked. Sometimes he would talk for fifteen to twenty minutes at a time. The principal's goal was to change Mr. A.'s behavior of talking for too long and to challenge him to present more meaningful information.

She could not approach Mr. A. with these two ideas because he would become too defensive and challenge her. Therefore, she would discuss the behavioral change from a student focus because Mr. A. would be less defensive and more likely to alter what happened in the classroom.

The Principal's Thinking about the Second Behavioral Change

The principal's second behavioral change centers on the lower-level quality of assignments in Mr. A.'s classes. She showed these assignments to another principal in town who had been a high school social studies teacher. Her colleague commented, "You've got to be kidding me. These papers are just rote memory worksheets. Our curriculum and assessments focus on analysis and other critical-thinking skills."

Again, Mrs. Y., the principal, had to determine how she could bring up this behavioral change without causing a defensive response. After thinking for a while, she came up with the idea of using the demands of the state testing as one reason for change. The data showed that the students at the high school had not made extensive progress in the essay portions of departmental assessments and the state test. The state test was administered in the late spring to tenth graders, and Mr. A. taught mostly tenth graders.

Mrs. Y. knew that she had to present this necessary change carefully. She did not want the teacher assigning lengthy social studies papers that were never read. She also knew that Mr. A. would need help in teaching the students to write about topics. Therefore, she determined that the desired behavioral change could, again, be filtered through students. Here is the core of message that the principal does *not* want to deliver:

> **Direct Message:** Mr. A., you need to reduce the amount of copying during class presentations and give students the opportunity to analyze important concepts and information—like they are required to do on the state tests.

In contrast, indirect behavior can be used with Mr. A. in order to get him to buy into the change. The filtered behavior is often an outcome of the actual desired change. In other words, if the teacher would agree to improve the quality of assignments and thinking skills from the start, then student written responses would improve. In essence, the administrator is starting with the outcome in order to achieve the desired behavioral change.

> **Indirect Message:** The students need to improve their higher-order thinking in written responses. These responses need go beyond factual knowledge from their notes to be analytical in nature—like items required on state exams.

Mrs. Y. knew that she did not want to mention the words *critical thinking* to the teacher because he believed students could not demonstrate higher-level thinking. Her hope was that the results of the new writing assignments would show the teacher that he had underestimated the potential of his students. Her communication begins with the *indirect message* and then provides a limited number of follow-up tasks. For example, the principal included this follow-up task, involving a colleague.

> Mrs. J. has developed a very structured approach to writing analytical paragraphs. She will share this step-by-step approach next Tuesday at your department meeting. It is important to try this approach and see if you have the same success as she does.

The principal has already talked to Mrs. J. about sharing the analytical writing steps. In addition, the principal knows that the teacher in question gets along well with Mrs. J.

The principal needed to decide if the message should be written or spoken. Given Mr. A.'s history, she decided to do both. She would hand carry the message to Mr. A.'s classroom immediately after school when students have left for the day. When handing the teacher the message, the principal would formally summarize the content of the message.

The Principal Now Involves the Entire Content Department

The principal's next task was to meet with the entire social studies department to reiterate the school goal of improving students' analysis, note taking, and analytical writing. The other teachers, except Mr. A., already engaged in these practices. However, the principal did not want one teacher to feel isolated because that would result in repetition of his defensive posture. So she met with the department to reiterate the same goals she shared with the teacher in question. She also included one new spoken idea that upgraded the instructional demand.

> **Principal's Addition:** The students will benefit if all written classroom tasks are scored by the next class. Student progress will be enhanced if, as a department, you can assign one short writing prompt a month to evaluate growth. Teachers for each course title can agree on a prompt that relates to the content.

This upgrade to the communication would push Mr. A. to initiate the analytical writing technique and require him to participate with the department.

> **Always remember . . .**
> The *indirect behavior* is the pragmatic vehicle that gets to the *desired behavioral change*. This process is necessary when the recipient of the message cannot handle the desired change and the principal needs to provide a more acceptable interim change.

Thinking More about the Principal's Indirect Approach

In this example, the principal used the indirect approach in order to increase the likelihood that the teacher would respond more positively to the message. In essence, this indirect statement becomes a filter through which the message recipient will process the rest of the message. Most people have an initial emotional reaction when they are addressed by authority figures. These emotions vary. The principal needs to keep in mind the following: What will be the recipient's emotional reaction to the message?

As already discussed, Mr. A. will react defensively unless he believes that the message is not antagonistic toward him as a teacher and person. With this in mind, the principal might begin her message by using key nouns that are more objective in nature. The administrator uses nouns such as *analysis*, *scores*, and *data* to begin the message.

> **Indirect Approach:** Based on an analysis of test scores, data shows that our students need to improve their performance. The quality of higher-order thinking skills demonstrated in student written responses is deficient. These responses need to go beyond the restatement of factual information.

The principal is using an *indirect approach* but still conveying the message. The principal is masking the message through the initial objective nouns. In essence, the message is conveying the idea that the data drives the need for action not the instructional practices of the teacher.

Here is what a *direct approach* to the start of the message might look like. This message "tells it like it is"; however, a direct, straightforward comment in this instance would likely bring about a defensive reaction from the teacher.

> Mr. A., you need to teach your students how to write analytical paragraphs. All you are doing now is asking students to list groups of facts in paragraphs. You need to reduce the amount of copying during class presentations and give students the

opportunity to analyze important concepts and information—like they are required to do on the state tests. This analysis needs to be incorporated into written classroom exercises.

If the principal began her message with this direct approach, the teacher would become extremely defensive, as had been the case in the past. The teacher's most likely response would be to say nothing to the principal and continue his current note-taking policy.

By starting the communication with an indirect approach, there is a greater likelihood that the teacher will be open to the message and act on some or all of the behavioral outcomes that need to take place. Here is part of the principal's action component of the message spoken to the teacher.

> **Spoken Comments to Teacher:** The district has begun placing a major emphasis on student note taking showing higher-order thinking. The district is requiring all administrators to look at samples of student work across different disciplines and grade levels. The notes from students must move beyond the fact level. With our goal of increasing students' critical thinking about the content, it is important that everyone in the department take another step. [Pause for teacher comment.]
>
> The mission statement for the district says that students need to be able to use higher-order thinking skills. Our school goal states that this objective will be met through note taking, class discussion, essay writing, and research projects. [Pause for teacher comment.]
>
> Mrs. J. has developed a very structured approach to writing analytical paragraphs. She will share this step-by-step approach next Tuesday at your department meeting. It is important to try this approach and see if you have the same success she does.

Always remember . . .
- If the recipient is dogmatic, the message needs to be less directive.
- If the recipient is more flexible, the message needs to be strong, but with more opportunity for the recipient to provide input.

Summary

1. The principal needs to think about the *person* with whom he or she is interacting. Especially important is the flexibility, friendliness, and professionalism of the individual.
2. The principal needs to think about past experiences with the message recipient.
3. The principal needs to incorporate a manageable number of outcomes in the message. The recipient should not become overwhelmed.
4. The principal needs to decide if he or she is going to use a *direct* or an *indirect* approach. The goal is to use the message type that will create the optimum emotional reaction in the recipient. Use this chart to think about the difference between the two approaches.

Comparing Direct and Indirect Approaches

Direct Approach	*Indirect Approach*
Each sentence presents the message in a focused, straightforward manner. The writer or speaker is not as concerned about the emotional reaction of the message recipient.	Each sentence places nouns in strategic locations to minimize a negative or defensive reaction. The writer or speaker does not want the emotional reaction of the message recipient to interfere with necessary actions.

4
Applying What You Have Learned

Exercises to Increase Understanding and Promote Discussion

As an administrator, you have to determine how the three factors of *flexibility*, *friendship*, and *professionalism* will influence your message. For example, if you need to get a nonnegotiable point across, you probably need to be less flexible. If you have to inform someone who is hostile toward you of a decision, you might not be friendly. You will always be professional, but there are times when a heightened need for caring might impact this professionalism.

Think of situations that match the levels of flexibility, friendship, and professionalism stated below:

The time I was inflexible and *did not* show a high level of friendship . . . (Example: I had to implement change with a teacher whom I had worked with for many years but who was resistant.)

_____
_____
_____

The time I was highly flexible and *did* show a high level of friendship . . . (Example: A teacher has not completed her yearly goal report because of a health issue, so I gave her a flexible deadline.)

_____
_____
_____

The time professionalism took priority over friendliness . . . (Example: Students were bullying another student in the class of a colleague who was not taking sufficient action. I directly intervened to stop the bullying and also privately reprimanded that teacher for his lack of action.)

_____
_____
_____

Now pretend to be a principal interacting with a science teacher who refuses to accept any responsibility for a significant problem. The science teacher and you are reviewing midterm exams and discover that the grades of her students are significantly below those of other sections of this course. The teacher states that many of these students "just do not seem to get it."

In this illustration, the teacher believes the following:

- The problem belongs to the students.
- Her curriculum is better than the new science curriculum that has been adopted because of an emphasis on comprehension.
- The teacher is not a highly flexible person.
- Sometimes the teacher tends to be sarcastic with students.

You, the principal, already know that the teacher is reluctant to change. Though she is not very flexible, the teacher is actually very friendly; she is not as professional as would be hoped. Your goal, after thinking about the attitude of the teacher, is to figure out the right structure of a message in order to have the desired behaviors occur.

How would you structure this message to the teacher?
_____
_____

Would you use a *direct* or *indirect approach?*_____

What might be the opening sentence of your spoken or written communication?
_____
_____

How would you tell the teacher that she has to be responsible for student performance?
_____
_____
_____
_____
_____
_____
_____
_____
_____
_____

Now think of a situation of your own where you need to communicate in writing with a teacher. You have to decide whether to employ a direct or an indirect approach.

Describe the situation._____
_____
_____
_____

Is this person flexible? _____

Is this person friendly? _____

Is this person professional? _____

Which approach do you choose? _____

Why did you make this choice? _____
_____

How would you begin the message? _____
_____
_____
_____

How would your language encourage the message recipient to change? _____
_____
_____
_____

Creating Your Own Case Study

Imagine a situation where you, as the principal, are going to interact with a teacher regarding a necessary instructional change. (If you have never been a principal before, use your own experience with principals to develop a valid case study.) You may decide on the particular instructional change for a particular curriculum and grade level. Choose your own levels of flexibility, friendship, and professionalism for yourself and the teacher with whom you are interacting.

Applying What You Have Learned / 47

Explain the specific instructional change you need implemented in the classroom of this teacher. The nature of the problem is revealed in your description.

_____
_____
_____
_____
_____

Describe the levels of flexibility, friendship and professionalism of the teacher involved in this situation.

Flexibility: _____

Friendship: _____

Professionalism: _____

Will the lead-in to your message be direct or indirect? Why did you make this choice?

_____
_____

Complete the following chart. First describe characteristics of the teacher you are focusing on in the center column. Then complete the left column of the chart. Finally, create the language of the direct or indirect approach to the message in the right column.

What are the *behaviors* the principal is looking for (what the principal wants to happen)?	Who is this *person* (what this person is like as an individual)?	As a result, what are the *tone* and *structure* of the message (how the principal needs to structure the message in order to create the best result)?
The outcome behaviors the principal would like to occur.	*What the principal knows to be true about the individual or group who will receive the message.*	

Analyzing Your Case Study

How did completing the chart on the previous page help you to determine the structure of the message you are going to give to the teacher?

_____
_____
_____

How difficult was it to determine the nature of the person in the middle column of your chart?

_____
_____

Describe why you chose the desired behavioral changes you listed in the left column.

_____
_____

Why did you decide to use a direct or indirect approach in your message?

_____
_____

Here is a hint to keep in mind. When communicating an important message, you may find it helpful to generate a list of important nouns that are essential to include in the message before you begin writing or prior to your meeting. To try out this idea, generate key nouns that you must include in your message. (You are going to write the actual message on the next page.)

_____   _____   _____
_____   _____   _____
_____   _____   _____

Chapter 4

Record the message you would send to the teacher in order to address the problem.

Part II

USING THE STRUCTURAL PYRAMID TO GET YOUR POINT ACROSS

5
Using the Subject as the Filter of Your Message

The Structural Pyramid

The Structural Pyramid is designed to help the administrator think about how to structure the message. In reality, a speaker or writer is not going to list possibilities related to each of these categories in the pyramid. However, by practicing the applications of each stage in the pyramid, your ability to apply the categories below automatically increases markedly.

Here are a few ideas to keep in mind as you learn about the pyramid:

- Keys nouns or pronouns in a sentence become a filter through which the rest of the message is processed.
- The verb communicates the degree of urgency in the message.
- The author needs to determine key questions that must be answered in order to get the point of the message across.
- The location of the dependent and independent clauses can either strengthen or soften the message.

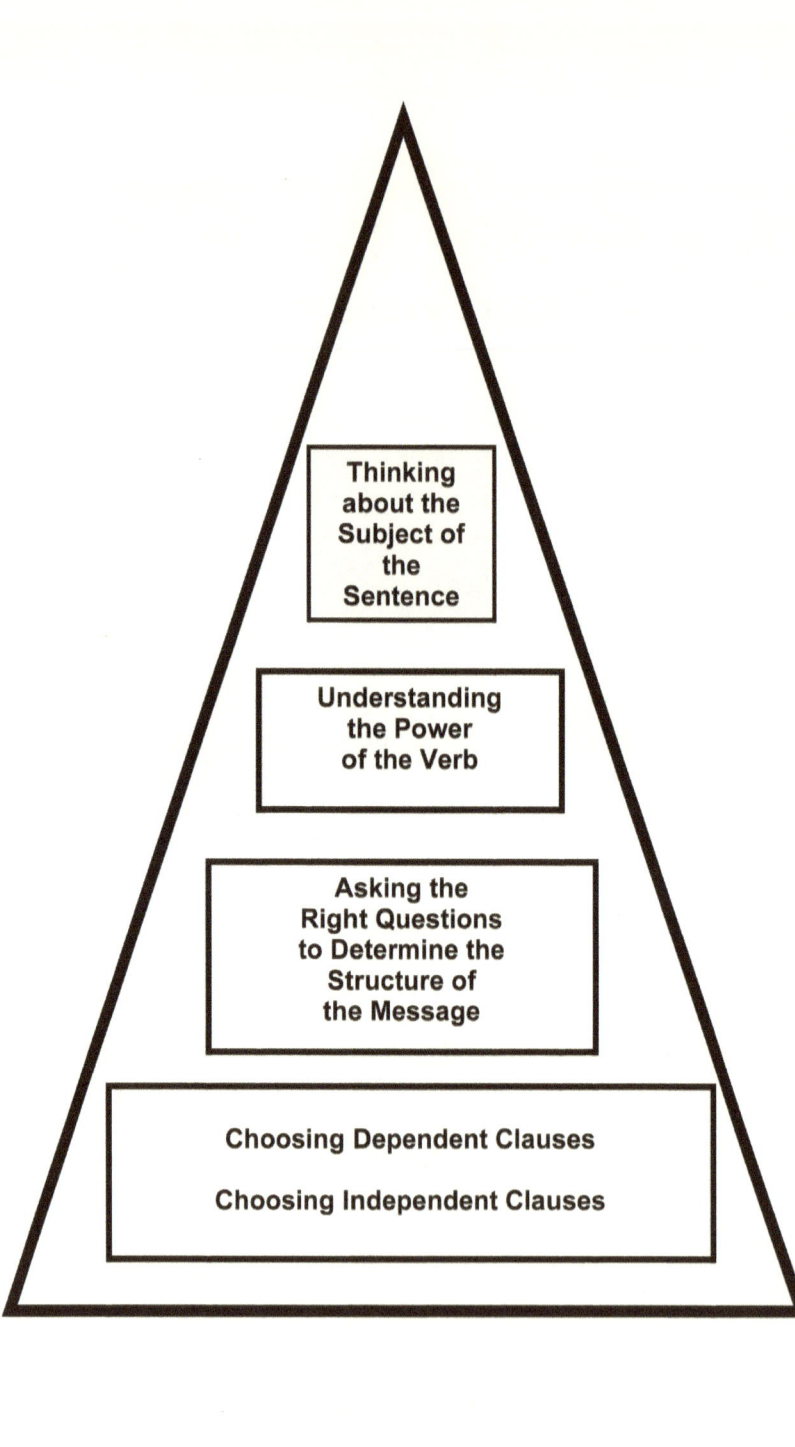

Category 1: Thinking about the Subject of the Sentence

In Grammar 101, the curriculum emphasizes the idea that the simple subject of the sentence is the noun or pronoun that receives the action of the verb. The simple subject becomes the filter through which the listener or reader comprehends the rest of the sentence.

Think about these two sentences stated to a teacher by an administrator. These sentences could be either written or spoken.

>**Sentence 1 (Option A):** Several *students* failed to pay attention during the lesson.

>**Sentence 1 (Option B):** *You* failed to notice that several students were not paying attention during the lesson.

Each of these sentences is similar in meaning. However, the filter of the first sentence is "students," while the filter of the second sentences is "you." In essence, the administrator is sending two different messages. In the first sentence, the primary burden of responsibility falls on the students with the secondary (implicit) responsibility falling on the teacher. In the second sentence, the opposite occurs. The primary responsibility is placed on the teacher with the students becoming a secondary focus.

In addition, it is essential to recognize that the verb *failed* appears in both sentences. Who failed? Did the students fail to pay attention? Or did the teacher fail to make sure that the students were paying attention.

The administrator needs to be aware of which primary focus he or she wants to communicate. Often the "person" being addressed becomes a determiner in this decision. If the teacher is highly defensive by nature, then the principal might choose sentence one below; he or she might add a second and third sentence that links the responsibility more directly to the teacher.

Sample One

Sentence 1: Several *students* failed to pay attention during the lesson.

Sentence 2: *I* observed two students sending notes, one student with his head down, and three looking at material from other classes.

Sentence 3: *You* need to make sure that the entire class remains focused on the lesson.

If the teacher is highly defensive, the administrator might still avoid the pronoun *you* as the subject and might use the third person in order to heighten receptivity by a listener or reader who does not want to hear or read anything negative. In addition, the subject *I* in the second sentence makes the principal the focus of the message. This may be the proper focus, or this pronoun might create an even greater defensive response from the teacher.

There is not a right or wrong subject for the sentences being communicated. *The goal is to create the best possible match of structure, recognizing the nature of the recipient's flexibility plus professionalism and the desired change of behavior.*

Here is a second sample sequence of subjects:

Sample Two

Sentence 1: Several *students* failed to pay attention during the lesson.

Sentence 2: Two *students* were sending notes, and one *student* had his head down. In addition, three *students* were looking at material from other classes.

Sentence 3: *Teachers* need to make sure that the entire class remains focused on the lesson.

Even though the messages contained in samples one and two are similar, the filters created by the subjects of the sentences cause the teacher to receive the message differently. Let's look at the second sentence from sample one and sample two.

Sample One

Sentence 2 (Option A): *I* observed two students sending notes, one student with his head down, and three looking at material from other classes.

Sample Two

Sentence 2 (Option B): Two *students* were sending notes, and one *student* had his head down. In addition, three *students* were looking at material from other classes.

The messages of both second sentences are almost the same. However, in sample one, the subject *I* places the filter on the behavior or action of the principal. If the teacher is defensive or if the teacher does not like the principal, then he or she will build walls that block out the actual purpose of the message. These walls promote negative messages of their own that inhibit beneficial communication. A defensive wall within the mind of the message recipient might say the following:

He really didn't see those students not paying attention. They were all listening. But he doesn't want to hear the truth.

To soften the teacher's reaction, the principal can eliminate the subject *I* and use *students* instead. This might not get rid of the entire defensive reaction, but "students" appears more objective.

The same concept applies to sentence three of each sample. The subject *you* in sentence three of sample one brings the focus of responsibility back to the teacher. In the second example, the focus of responsibility is to all teachers.

Sample One

Sentence 3 (Option A): *You* need to make sure that the entire class remains focused on the lesson.

Sample Two

Sentence 3 (Option B): *Teachers* need to make sure that the entire class remains focused on the lesson.

By comparing the subjects in these three sentences, you can recognize the differences in the filters of the message.

	Subjects	
	Sample One	Sample Two
Sentence 1	students	students
Sentence 2	I	students
Sentence 3	you	(all) teachers

The choice of the simple subject of the sentence's independent clause will have an impact on the receptivity of the listener or reader. Again, there is no right or wrong choice. The goal is to *match* the subjects of the message to the personality (or person) of the teacher. Obviously, this matching process is not going to be perfect. Without doubt, the administrator might misjudge the best filters needed to optimize the impact of the message. However, being conscious of this idea is critical.

In reality, the administrator is *not* going to spend an inordinate amount of time listing possible subjects. However, by being tuned into the idea of subject selection, the administrator can become increasingly competent at making choices that improve the receptivity of the listener or reader.

Always remember . . .
The recipient must comprehend the message in the way you intend it to be communicated, or there can be negative consequences.

Using *It* as the Subject

The subject of the sentence is selected to clarify meaning for the reader. The word *it* as the subject minimizes this clarification.

Situation 1

Example with *It*: *It* was noted that six of your third period students were in the hall five minutes after the bell rang this past Monday.

The component "It was noted" is vague. The reader is not certain what "it" refers to. Obviously, someone observed this situation, and there is a reasonable chance that the reader or listener will challenge the statement with the question by asking who it was.

The administrator may not want to implicate the real observer (who may have requested anonymity). In this instance, the administrator would begin the statement with the focus on the difficulty. If the teacher pushes for the name of the staff member, the principal could say that the name is not important.

Example without *It*: Six students from your third period class were making noise in the hallway next to your classroom last Monday after the third period bell sounded. All of these students were part of your third period class. The important idea is that students cannot be in the halls when they are supposed to be in class.

Situation 2

A second problem with the word *it* as the subject is that the real center of the message gets moved to a subordinate clause. The significant component of the message below is in the subordinate clause beginning with the word *that*. The first part of the sentence, or the independent clause, is nebulous. As a result, the filter created by the subject *it* is of no positive value. In fact, certain listeners might not even pay attention to the message after the words "It was noted . . ."

Example with *It*: It was noted *that six of your third period students* were in the hall five minutes after the bell rang this past Monday.

Sometimes, when the dependent clause becomes the independent clause, the strength of the message increases.

Example without *It*: *Six students from your third period* class were making noise in the hallway next to your classroom last Monday after the third period bell sounded.

Situation 3

If the administrator is praising the teacher, he or she needs to place the positive actions out front.

Example with *It*: It is important to recognize the hard work of Mrs. Jones, who organized last night's successful PTA dinner. Mrs. Jones, take a bow.

In this instance, the positive action is clear, but the subject *it* weakens the statement.

Example without *It*: Mrs. Jones's hard work and remarkable organization skills are the primary reasons why last night's PTA dinner was so successful. Mrs. Jones, take a bow.

Situation 4

The administrator at other times may want to be vague on purpose. This is especially beneficial if he or she does not want to point the finger at someone because incremental follow-up action is going to occur. In this instance, the administrator should use one of these three sentence beginnings.

It is essential . . .
It is necessary . . .
It is important . . .

With each of these three beginnings, the primary focus of the message does become subordinate in meaning. However, the administrator might wish to initiate the message in this purposely vague manner because the issue is controversial. Therefore, the lesser degree of strength is designed to plant a seed that the administrator will nourish continuously.

Example One with *It*: It is essential that students receive corrected quizzes within two instructional days.

This issue might be controversial among staff members who find this time frame unreasonable. The sentence does not use the word *teachers* for this reason. The administrator could have stated the following:

Example Two without *It*: Teachers need to return corrected student quizzes within two instructional days.

Or if school policy exists, he or she could have rephrased the statement as follows:

Example Three without *It*: School board policy states that the teacher must return corrected student quizzes within two instructional days.

How could the different subjects influence the reaction of the message recipients, the teachers? The reaction to *example one* would tend to be the weakest of the three. Some teachers who do not follow this policy might say, "Yeah, yeah, yeah," to themselves. Some teachers might figure that the administrator is obligated to make this statement. The administrator could use this manipulation of language purposely to generate a point that will receive a lot of follow-up.

The reaction to example two will be stronger than the first example. The subject is teachers. Those who do not adhere to the policy would hear this statement as a directive. The administrator is presenting the notion that he or she is directly responsible for this statement.

The reaction to example three would tend to be strong as well. The difference is that the subject now becomes "school board policy," which indicates that the administrator is carrying out a policy from the school board. This example takes the responsibility of initiation away from the administrator, who still possesses the responsibility of enforcement. Which of these examples should the administrator use?

62 / Chapter 5

The choice of sentence structure goes back to the collective personalities of the listeners or readers. If the administrator knows that the recipients of the message will react with hostility, then he or she might choose examples one or three. The choice of message structure goes back to the principal's diagnosis of the message recipient's flexibility, friendliness, and professionalism.

Situation 5

Often the speaker or writer needs to include a second component exploring why. The why component always goes back to the subject of the independent clause. A look at the previous three examples illustrates this point.

> **Example One with *It*:** It is essential that students receive corrected quizzes within two instructional days.
>
> **Why Question:** Why is it essential that students receive corrected quizzes within two days?
>
> **Example Two without *It*:** Teachers need to return corrected student quizzes within two instructional days.
>
> **Why Question:** Why do teachers need to return the corrected quizzes within two instructional days?
>
> **Example Three without *It*:** School board policy states that the teacher must return corrected student quizzes within two instructional days.
>
> **Why Question:** Why does school policy state that the teacher must return corrected quizzes within two instructional days?

Each of these three questions will generate slightly different answers. The first response will center on the students, the second on teacher responsibility, and the third response on the reason for this school board policy. Here are the three examples plus the "why" responses:

> **Example One with *Why*:** It is essential that students receive corrected quizzes within two instructional days. Students need

this corrected work in order to determine areas of strength and weakness for future studying.

Example Two with *Why*: Teachers need to return corrected student quizzes within two instructional days. Teachers give these quizzes in order to evaluate student learning. If too much time has gone between the day of the quiz and when the quiz is returned, the quiz's diagnostic value is diminished significantly.

Example Three with *Why*: School policy states that the teacher must return corrected student quizzes within two instructional days. A school board task force studied this matter two years ago. Based on interviews with teachers, students, and parents, as well as studying educational research, board members established this policy. A copy of their report is available in the office.

Asking the Recipient "Why?"

When speaking, the power of the message is often increased markedly by asking the listener or listeners to tell *you* why the stated idea seems so important. This strategy pushes the recipient to think through the meaning of the message. Often, if the listener can arrive at a valid explanation of the principal's statement, the buy-in to the desired behavior is accomplished. If the listener cannot generate a "why" response to the statement by the principal, then the principal can provide the explanation that was originally intended. Let's use example three to illustrate this point.

The principal says: "School board policy states that the teacher must return corrected student quizzes within two instructional days."

The principal asks the listener: "Why do you think this idea is important?"

If the listener can give a valid reason why, then the content of the message has sunk in and the likelihood of acceptance is great. If the listener cannot give a reasonable response, then the principal continues with what he or she was going to say anyway.

Avoid Implying Criticism

If the principal presented a message to all teachers during a faculty meeting or through an e-mail and the message was really intended to change the behavior of a small number of teachers, the other teachers might feel insulted. In this instance, the principal must deliver the message only to those it is intended for.

Here are two illustrations:

> **Example One:** Teachers need to return corrected student quizzes within two instructional days. (Delivered to whole faculty at meeting.)
>
> **Example Two:** Teachers need to return corrected student quizzes within two instructional days. (Delivered to one teacher during a principal/teacher conference.)

Let's use these two examples to think about the idea of matching the message to the right audience.

Background Information

Ms. S. is the principal of a school with fifty faculty members. School board policy requires that quizzes be returned to students within two instructional days. Six teachers are consistently delinquent in following this policy. The principal is aware of the problem because it was even discussed at a PTO meeting that the principal attended. Through informal follow-up discussions with students, Ms. S. confirmed that a few teachers kept quizzes for a week or more before returning them to students.

> **Example One:** Teachers need to return corrected student quizzes within two instructional days. (Delivered to whole faculty at meeting.)

From the principal's point of view: Ms. S. knew that she had to correct this problem. She decided that the most expedient way to deliver the message was to bring up the issue at a faculty meeting.

Teacher reaction: After the meeting, several excellent teachers met with her in her office and explained that they were insulted by her message and that if there was a problem with a few teachers, she should speak to them directly.

> **Example Two:** Teachers need to return corrected student quizzes within two instructional days. (Delivered to one teacher during a principal/teacher conference.)

From the principal's point of view: Ms. S. knew that she had to correct this problem. She decided that the most effective way to deliver the message to the teachers who needed to hear it was to speak to each one privately. At each of these individual meetings, she stated the need for correcting within the required time span.

Teacher reaction: In this instance, some of the teachers addressed understood the message and other reacted negatively. However, teachers who were already adhering to district policy were not offended.

Analysis

With example one, an atmosphere of resentment may develop among the faculty. In addition, expert faculty members may begin to question the leadership of this principal. These teachers could get the idea that the principal is afraid to confront people directly.

In example two, the principal communicates directly with each teacher who is not following the policy and makes the expectation of compliance clear to those teachers who need to improve their performance.

> **Keep this rule in mind:**
> Principals need to determine their audience prior to structuring and delivering the message.

Always remember these two important conclusions.

A message delivered to the wrong audience is a message in itself!

A message sent is not necessarily the message received.

Exercises to Increase Understanding and Promote Discussion

This section emphasizes the importance of the choice of subject in your communication. Read each pair of statements below. Identify and circle the noun or pronoun that is the simple subject (filter) of each sentence. Then determine how the subject influences the meaning.

Tuesday's meeting will focus on problems with the new mathematics program.

Problems with the new mathematics program will be the primary focus at Tuesday's meeting.

Comment Statement 1 _____

Comment Statement 2 _____

Only one teacher and five parents attended the last parent and teacher meeting.

Attendance at the last parent and teacher meeting was poor with only one teacher and five parents present.

Comment Statement 1 _____

Comment Statement 2 _____

Using the Subject as the Filter of Your Message / 67

Teachers have worked very hard to increase proficiency in writing, and the results show it.

Your hard work to increase student proficiency in writing has led to noticeably positive results.

Comment Statement 1 _____

Comment Statement 2 _____

Students are not citing sources properly in their research papers.

Student failure to cite source properly is a significant issue.

Comment Statement 1 _____

Comment Statement 2 _____

Take a look at some of the memos, e-mails, and letters you have written during the past few months. Then select three important sentences from the messages that you believe have strong subjects (nouns or pronouns). Rewrite these sentences below.

Sentences with strong subjects	**Why subject is strong**
1. _____ _____	_____ _____
2. _____ _____	_____ _____
3. _____ _____	_____ _____

68 / Chapter 5

Next select two sentences from your memos, e-mails, or letters that you believe would have been better with a different subject. Change the subject to improve the message.

1. Sentence with weak subject: _____

_____

This subject is weak because _____

Sentence with new subject: _____

_____

2. Sentence with weak subject _____

_____

This subject is weak because _____

Sentence with new subject: _____

_____

Read the following case study and write an e-mail to the designated audience.

> Teachers from all grade levels have worked hard to create outstanding bulletin boards containing student writing. A district goal over the past two years has been to improve student writing across the curricula and to display many examples of student work that show models of effective writing. Teachers have accomplished these goals consistently. The most recent bulletin boards around the hallways of the school were the best yet.
>
> Visitors from another school district commented to the principal about how enthusiastic and proud the students were regarding their writing displayed in the classrooms and hall bulletin boards. In addition, both the superintendent and influential parents have made similar comments. Throughout the school year, the principal has carefully monitored these displays and facilitated discussion about student work at many team meetings. The principal appreciates the extra time and effort it has taken the teachers to create such effective displays.

Using the Subject as the Filter of Your Message / 69

The principal knows most teachers have worked hard to share student work in the best possible way. In addition, most teachers take pride in student accomplishments. The teachers organize opportunities for students to travel around the school looking at bulletin boards. The teachers, in general, have been very flexible and professional in this area. They often put up bulletin board displays after school.

The principal wants to praise the teachers for their hard work and dedication.

Create a five- to six-sentence memorandum to faculty members providing positive feedback for their good work. Be sure to use subjects that create the correct filters. Hint: Remember that this memo is about the teachers' hard work and not about the principal.

_____
_____
_____
_____
_____

Review the memo you created praising the teachers. Locate the simple subject for each sentence. Then evaluate how the subject provides a strong filter that conveys your message.

List the Simple Subject Filter	How Does This Filter Shape the Message?
Sentence 1: _____	_____
Sentence 2: _____	_____
Sentence 3: _____	_____
Sentence 4: _____	_____
Sentence 5: _____	_____
Sentence 6: _____	_____

Read the following case study and write an e-mail to the designated audience.

> The school board is committed to establishing a strong Response to Intervention Program. Each school in the district is revising its "child study team" procedures to require that teachers bring hard data, including graphs of student performance, to child study team meetings. Four teachers have attended these meetings with folders of student work but no analysis of student work or graphs of student progress. The principal, who attends each of these meetings, has spoken to each of these teachers previously; however, the teachers continue to come to these meeting without the required information.
>
> These four teachers have resisted change in the past. They tend to nod their heads at the meetings, but they make no modifications in their classrooms. When the teachers are called upon at meetings, they tend to speak in generalities that have little diagnostic value. When other members of the child study team" initiate diagnostic information, these four teachers do not seem interested.
>
> In this instance, the principal has decided to speak with each of the four teachers individually. Prior to speaking, the principal thinks about levels of teacher flexibility and professionalism in order to help him organize his message. The principal also has to decide if he is going to use a direct or indirect approach to the initiation of his comments.

Respond to the items below. (You can relate this case study to actual colleagues with whom you have worked.)

Write a couple of sentences describing the flexibility of one of the teachers to be addressed.

_____
_____
_____

Write a couple of sentences describing the professionalism of this teacher.

_____
_____
_____

Using the Subject as the Filter of Your Message / 71

Create three or four of the sentences to be shared during the meeting with this teacher. Circle the simple subject in each of these sentences.

Sentence 1: _____

Sentence 2: _____

Sentence 3: _____

Sentence 4: _____

List the Simple Subject Filter	How Does This Filter Shape the Message?
Sentence 1: _____	_____
Sentence 2: _____	_____
Sentence 3: _____	_____
Sentence 4: _____	_____

What is one conclusion you can draw about your selections of appropriate filters in the sentences you write and speak?

_____
_____
_____
_____
_____

72 / Chapter 5

Read the following case study and write a paragraph to the designated audience.

> Recently there has been a fire drill near the end of a school day. The principal has observed that six classes were not following the fire drill guidelines. In two classes the students were talking as they moved down the hall. In three classes the students were both talking and not leaving the building in a line. One class exited the building at least two minutes after the rest of the students; the principal observed that all of the students in this class were wearing the jackets they brought to school and were carrying their backpacks.

Who is the audience? Why have you chosen this audience?

_____

_____

If the principal were going to speak to the responsible teachers, should he or she speak to them as a group or one at a time? Or should the principal address the issue with the entire faculty?

_____

_____

Why does the principal not have to spend time assessing the levels of flexibility and professionalism of the teachers involved in this situation?

_____

_____

Create a four- to five-sentence paragraph addressing this issue.

_____

_____

_____

_____

Using the Subject as the Filter of Your Message / 73

Review your message and locate the simple subject for each sentence.

List the Simple Subject Filter	How Does This Filter Shape the Message?
Sentence 1: _____	_____
Sentence 2: _____	_____
Sentence 3: _____	_____
Sentence 4: _____	_____
Sentence 5: _____	_____

Case Study Analysis

Think about the similarities and differences among the three case studies presented in these exercises. Discuss these similarities and differences below.

Similarities: _____
_____
_____
_____
_____

Differences: _____
_____
_____
_____

6

Making the Verb the Engine of Your Message

Category 2: The Power of the Verb

As a high school English teacher might say, the verb expresses the action in the sentence. However, when communicating, the significance of the verb is even greater. The verb really represents the power of the message. The choice of verb will have an impact on whether the message produces desirable results.

Think about the verb in this statement.

> Student performance on the Biology Advanced Placement Test fails to meet the expectations of the school board and the central administration.

The word *fails* is the key verb in the above statement. The listener or reader uses the verb to draw a conclusion about the strength of the message. *Fail* creates a clear indication that the person (or group) presenting the message is not pleased. This verb will cause the listener or reader to generate a strong inner or external response. An inner response takes place within the mind of the individual, and an external response is spoken or written to others.

Sample Inner Response: I work as hard as anyone. I spend so much time trying to help these students do well on the AP test. If they don't like the results, let's see if they can find someone else.

Sample External Response: Personally, I am pleased with our AP results. Last year I compared our scores to other districts. In some cases we do better. The other AP teacher and I have worked hard. I think the idea of failing is totally bogus.

The administrator must determine what type of response he or she wants from the individual or group. Is the goal to motivate? To challenge? To frustrate the listener or reader so that he or she will drop out? Is the goal constructive?

The verb expresses the certainty of the writer's message. By using the verb *fails*, the administrator is certain or convinced of the validity of the message. If the administrator were not as convinced, he or she might use a different verb.

Student *performance* on the Biology Advanced Placement Test *does not meet* the expectation of the school board and central administration.

The response by the listener or reader might be similar as described above, but the depth of feeling between communicator and recipient is not as pronounced.

The filter of the subject ("performance"), plus the power of the verb ("does not meet"), induces a personal reaction that leads to a response. Every message is designed to elicit a response. By choosing the appropriate subject (filter) and the optimum verb (power), the administrator will have a better chance of eliciting the desired response.

Case Study Showing the Filter of the Subject and the Power of the Verb

How does the choice of subject and verb help to emphasize the desired change? Here is one example that shows possible answers to these questions.

Imagine a principal was meeting with a fifth grade teacher after watching that teacher work with a group of students in the classroom to improve comprehension of mathematics content. The principal observed that the teacher spent 80 percent of instructional time talking to the students. The principal had previously discussed the importance of group interaction with the teacher. After the observation, the principal stated the following to the teacher.

> I observed that you spent 80 percent of the time talking to the students, and the students were actively involved only about 10 percent of the time.

Here is some of the principal's thinking:

- **What does the principal see as the issue?** The principal hopes that the teacher will change her instructional behavior from teacher-dominant to more student-participatory instruction. The current learning environment does not encourage students to interact with either the teacher or other students. The principal realizes that this teacher is rather insecure and dogmatic by nature.
- **What does history tell the principal about this scenario?** The administrator has previously intervened with minimal success. The administrator has expressed concern about too much teacher talk during this teacher's lessons. Having observed the same pattern of teacher dominance during the recently observed lesson, the principal realizes that change is going to be difficult.
- **How does the choice of subject and verb help to get the point across?** *I* is the filter and *observed* is the verb of the independent clause. By starting with "I," the focus is on the principal's behavior, and the teacher's behavior has a subordinate position in the statement. If the principal wants the teacher's behavior to be the focus, then the principal's statement could be, "You spent 80 percent of the time talking to the students, and the students were actively involved only about 10 percent of the time."

However, if the principal wants the filter of the message to be the students, he or she could say "The students participated actively only 10 percent of the time during the lesson." Here the filter is *students* and the verb is *participated*.

The principal chooses the filter and the verb according to the desired impact on the teacher. The communicator always needs to remember this: the choice of sentence structure must produce a response from the teacher that benefits students because students are the bottom line in education.

Using the Verb as the Engine

The verb usually is the lead-in to the predicate of the sentence. This means that all language following the verb is connected. The verb becomes the engine that pushes the rest of the language in the statement. Not every sentence is designed to drive home a point because some sentences are more important than others. For example:

> The teacher contract *states* that every teacher *must complete* six hours of independent work over the summer vacation. The teacher contract specifies that the building administrator must approve the goals and objectives of this independent work prior to the last day of school in June.

The verbs in the first sentence above are *states* and *must complete*. These verbs are extremely important because they relate to previously agreed upon language that impacts the job of the school staff.

The verb *states* drives the subordinate clause, "that every teacher must complete six hours of independent work over the summer vacation." The verb *must complete* drives the predicate of the dependent clause, "six hours of independent work over the summer vacation."

Why does this matter? The fact that the contract "states" specific language propels the reader to take the rest of sentence seriously. The filter of the sentence is "teacher contract" and the power is "state." If this sentence were written or spoken with a weaker verb, the reader or listener might not pay as much attention to the overall message. For example:

> The teacher contract indicates that every teacher should complete six hours of independent work over the summer vacation.

The verb *indicates* is not as definitive as "states." The helping verb *should* implies an option, while the helping verb *must* creates a certainty. As a result, the reader or listener will view the message as weaker and, therefore, not treat the content of the message as seriously. If the administrator is after a group response, then the immediate reaction of the few might influence the total reaction of the group.

For example, if the administrator uses the verbs *indicates* and *should*, a small number of veteran teachers might not treat the message with respect. Their comments to others could create a laissez-faire attitude among the entire group. This result would create a huge headache for the administrator, who is probably responsible for approving the summer work.

Message recipients sometimes react negatively to strong verbs. This is especially true of individuals who do not like being told what to do. Within most groups, there are always a few hostile individuals who look for excuses to be negative. These people tend to want others to join them in their negativity. The administrator has to cut the negative responses of these individuals off at the pass.

If the administrator chooses the helping word *must*, then the selection of the subject from the independent clause becomes significant. For example:

> The *teacher contract* states that every teacher must complete six hours of independent work over the summer vacation.

The simple subject of the independent clause in this example is *contract*, which is attached to the word *teacher*. That the administrator is citing the teacher contract makes this message more palatable to a hostile reader or listener.

80 / Chapter 6

In the sentence below, the administrator does not use "teacher contract" as the filter. Consequently, a hostile recipient might not receive this component of the message as positively. Instead, the administrator begins the sentence with "The building administrator..." Therefore, the filter shifts from the teacher contract to the building administrator. This could be true even if the implication that the contract also states this information is fair to assume. For example:

> The *building administrator* must approve the goals and objectives of this independent work prior to the last day of school in June.

The hostile recipient of the message could grumble to him or herself, "Who does this principal think he is?"

In this example, the negative recipient is hearing that the administrator is giving the orders, not the teacher contract. For example:

> The *teacher contract* states that the *building administrator* must approve the goals and objectives of this independent work prior to the last day of school in June.

> **Always remember...**
> The subject and verb of the independent clause work as a team to heighten the recipient's acceptance of the message.

The Inner versus External Response

Each time someone communicates, you will have an inner response. The inner response refers to the emotional reaction you have to the message. This reaction varies, depending on many factors, such as who states the message and what your prior experience with this individual is. The inner response precedes the external one. An external response can be reflected in statements, posture, or facial expressions. Usually, the inner response will have some control over the external response.

Making the Verb the Engine of Your Message / 81

Exercises to Increase Understanding and Promote Discussion

This exercise is designed to explore the idea of an inner and an external response. Think about an educational message that you have received recently from someone above you on the leadership hierarchy.

The message was about _____

My *inner response* to the message was _____
_____

Why did you have this inner response? _____
_____

My *external response* to the message was _____
_____

Why did you have this external response? _____
_____

How are the internal and external responses different? _____
_____

How are the internal and external responses similar? _____
_____

82 / Chapter 6

What impact did your inner response have on your external response?

_____
_____
_____

Locate one sentence from the memo, letter, or report that generated a strong *inner response*. Tell why you think this response occurred.

This response occurred because _____
_____
_____

My internal response did/did not surprise me because _____
_____
_____

What conclusions can you draw about the relationships between internal and external responses?

_____
_____
_____

An official from the Board of Health might write the statements below as part of a longer health inspection report. Which statement do you think would be the better message? The recipient of the message is the restaurant owner.

Statement A: I observed trays of raw meat in the corridor next to the kitchen.

Statement B: Trays of raw meat were stacked up in the corridor next to the kitchen.

I think statement __ would be the more effective sentence because

_____

Making the Verb the Engine of Your Message / 83

Pretend this same Board of Health inspector observed an employee blowing his nose in the kitchen and not washing his hands. How would the inspector communicate this in the report? After writing, circle each simple subject and underline each verb. Then share why you chose those subjects and verbs with a colleague.

_____
_____
_____

Consider this statement from earlier in this chapter: the filter of the subject, plus the power of the verb, induces a personal reaction that leads to a response. Draw a picture showing the relationships expressed in this statement.

For this exercise, think about an instructional behavior that you would like a teacher to change. Once you come up with this situation, answer the questions below.

What do you see as the issue? _____
_____

Why is this an issue? _____
_____

How does your history with this person impact your communication? _____
_____
_____
_____

How are you going to use the best subject and verb to get your point across? _____
_____
_____
_____

Are you going to use a direct or an indirect beginning to your message? Why? _____
_____
_____
_____

Choose a memo, letter, or report that you have written. The selected communication must contain one paragraph of at least four sentences. Find the verbs in the paragraph and list them below. Include helping verbs with main verbs. For example:

> You must record students' attendance every day, and then you must send that information to the office.

There are two verbs in this sentence, *record* and *send*, each with a helping verb, *must*. Record the verbs from your message below.

Sentence 1 verbs _____ _____ _____

Sentence 2 verbs _____ _____ _____

Sentence 3 verbs _____ _____ _____

Sentence 4 verbs _____ _____ _____

Sentence 5 verbs _____ _____ _____

Evaluate these verbs. Do the verbs represent the "right" amount of power? Are there any verbs that you would change?
_____
_____
_____

Select one sentence where you would want to strengthen the verb. Rewrite that sentence below.
_____
_____

Using the Verb to Encourage Problem Solving

Joint decision making creates a positive school environment. Obviously, the administrator cannot engage in this type of interaction all of the time. He or she must finalize certain decisions without the consent or input of faculty. However, some of the time a conscious effort to work as a team produces a positive attitude among the staff.

When joint decision making is the goal, the administrator needs to communicate the purpose of this venture clearly. The staff must comprehend that the problem-solving process is not just an exercise with the administrator making the final choice anyway. Initial communication is essential for a successful interaction. Central to this initiation is the verb choice of the administrator.

The effectiveness of the principal's initial message will have a huge impact on the staff's interest and willingness to participate actively in the decision-making process. This experience is a perfect time for the principal to think about the collective flexibility, friendship, and professionalism of the faculty.

- How well does the group get along?
- How well does the collective group respond to change?
- What is/are the most important desired change(s)?
- How will the collective group work to solve problems?

Based on the responses to these questions, the administrator can ask him or herself the following: How do I structure my message so that the faculty will take it seriously and be motivated to work as a team? What verbs am I going to use in order to structure this motivating message? How am I going set up the meeting room to facilitate interaction?

The way you structure the initial message will have an impact on the motivation of the entire group. The administrator might have determined that this exercise has two purposes: first to resolve the issue, and second to give members of the faculty who do not speak with each other an opportunity to interact. The principal must decide if the collective group will respond better to a direct or indirect message initiation.

Getting Ready for Collegial Problem Solving

In order to move forward with this thinking process, the administrator responds to the questions about collective flexibility, friendship, and professionalism of the faculty. These responses can be jotted down or inside his or her head. These responses will enable the principal to prepare for the interaction with staff.

- **How well does the group get along?** The group has three definable cliques of four to six people. There is a general cordiality.
- **How well does the collective group respond to change?** One clique is inflexible and does not like change. The rest of the staff accept change.
- **What is/are the most important desired change(s)?** The staff needs to enhance the quality of communication with parents regarding daily assignments and student progress. Currently, there are no defined policies, and approaches to communicating with parents are very different.
- **How will the collective group work to solve problems?** The staff needs to define the problem in language that everyone accepts. Then they have to think about possible methods for solving the issue. Finally, the staff needs to create a policy document that each staff member signs.

The actual setup of the room will have an impact on the comfort and commitment of the group. The organization of the listening space will impact the recipients' attitudes as the administrator shares the initial message. In addition, the setup of the room dictates a sense of purpose and promotes the type of language desired. Therefore, the administrator asks one more preliminary question.

- **How am I going set up the meeting room to facilitate interaction?** The room will be set up for groups. I will define seating to ensure that cliques do not sit together. I will create a simple rationale for the makeup of each group.

Based on the responses to these questions, the administrator can ask him or herself the following:

- **How do I structure my initial message so that the faculty will take it seriously and be motivated to work as a team?** The message needs both a direct and an indirect approach. It will start out with an indirect approach that centers on the benefit to students of a well-define policy. Once the group agrees to this statement, the initial message will be a direct statement that a problem exists. I am not going to define the problem for the staff, but I have to make sure the parameters of the problem are understood.
- **What verbs am I going to use in order to structure this motivating message?** With the indirect portion of the message, I will use very strong verbs in order to get the significance of the problem across. With the direct portion of the message, I will use both strong verbs and the lead-in "It is essential . . ."

Case Study about Collaborative Decision Making

The following is a sample issue for collaborative decision making by the faculty of a middle school.

What the Principal Knows

Dr. J. is the principal of a regional middle school in a rural area. Some students live forty miles from the school and face an hour commute each morning. Dr. J. has been reviewing student test scores in reading, writing, and mathematics for the current school year and has noticed a decline in all three areas from the previous year. For the two school years prior to the current one, test scores had increased by an average of four percent.

She has discussed this matter with the school department heads, selected teachers, and the central administration. These individuals did not have any specific reasons for the decline. Dr.

J. has tried, without success, to think about extenuating circumstances that might cause the decline.

What the Principal Decides to Do

The principal was very concerned because her school had worked hard to prepare for the state tests. The central administration was also disappointed and made it clear that a plan of action was necessary. Ordinarily, Dr. J. would have met with a few trusted teachers and formulated a plan to correct the downslide for the following school year. However, she decided to take a different tack.

Dr. J. determined that a more serious plan for implementation would occur if the entire faculty agreed upon specific steps. Thus she decided to use her professional development day at the end of year to initiate a plan for the next fall.

Setting Up for Collegial Problem Solving

Prior to the in-service day, Dr. J. thought about the questions that would help her reflect upon the collective flexibility, friendship, and personality of the staff.

- **How well does the group get along?** Most teachers are polite, but they are not overly friendly with each other. There is one clique of four teachers that tends to dominate the decision making of others.
- **How well does the collective group respond to change?** Most teachers are not highly flexible. Many resent the emphasis placed on testing. Many try to avoid change by closing their doors and doing what they have always done. Every change, no matter how small, is a major undertaking.
- **What is/are the most important desired change(s)?** Teachers will work in groups to come up with a plan to infuse testing tasks into the curriculum. Teachers will take the plan seriously. Each teacher will follow a prescribed series

of exercises that will improve performance on one designated test.
- **How will the collective group work to solve problems?** Members of the faculty who do not usually talk will work together. Groups of teachers will convince others of ideas. Teachers will learn test objectives and test items; then they will relate item types to the curriculum.

Based on her responses to these questions, the Dr. J. asked herself the following:

- **How do I structure my initial message so that the faculty will take it seriously and be motivated to work as a team?** Some faculty resent the emphasis placed on state testing and are vocal. They also are sensitive to the implication that it is "the teachers' fault." The language needs to focus on the "we" and on "our" curriculum. The teachers need to become more data-driven. Therefore, I clearly need to create an *indirect approach* to the initiation of the message.
- **How am I going set up the meeting room to facilitate interaction?** The tables where people will sit have to be arranged to foster group interaction. I will establish a clear purpose for the meeting. I will determine the makeup of each group and work with staff to set clear tasks (for example, reviewing students' past results for areas of strength and listing areas in need of improvement). I will also assign specific roles to group members (such as facilitator and recorder).

Reflecting on the Principal's Own Flexibility, Friendship, and Professionalism

Dr. J. knows that she is a structured person and cannot surrender that behavior entirely. But she understands that she needs to change her behavior somewhat to accomplish her goal of a united faculty commitment. So Dr. J. thinks about how she can be more flexible.

As Dr. J. reflects upon her flexibility, she realizes that it is essential to involve the five department leaders prior to meeting with the faculty. She knows that she needs to work with those leaders to analyze test data so that they can collaborate in leading the school's efforts to improve performance.

Ordinarily, Dr. J. would select herself to share test results with the staff. However, because she has considered her flexibility, she knows this is one area that requires a surrendering of control.

Dr. J. also thinks about the idea of friendship. Does her view of friendship and her existing friendships with the faculty have a potential impact on the receptivity to the message? After careful thought, she determines that friendship has limited or no real impact. Dr. J. is not close friends with any of the department chairpeople, but there is no antagonistic relationship either. Generally, these chairpeople are willing to listen, even if three of the five tend to be reluctant to implement any major change.

Finally, the principal quickly thinks about her attitude toward professionalism. She concludes that this is not a factor.

Dr. J. draws one conclusion from her self-analysis: "I need to modify and carefully monitor my flexibility; I need to make sure that I do not dominate, but that I lead.

Some of Dr. J.'s Introductory Words to the Faculty

Teachers need to recognize the urgency of the situation:

> Our school received the data from the state tests two weeks ago. The department leaders and I have reviewed those data and found a decline in student performance in most areas of reading, writing, and mathematics.

(At this point, the department leaders share the results of the state tests.)

The entire building needs to ensure that student performance is maximized:

> Student performance is our most important mission. One of our responsibilities is helping our students gain the knowledge

and skills they need to be successful on the state tests. As a faculty, we need to determine the factors contributing to our declining scores on the state tests. We have successfully tackled problems with student performance before, and we can do it again. Some areas to investigate could include our curricula, our tests and assessments, and our instructional strategies.

Response to anticipated resentment by some teachers toward the state testing:

The department leaders have created a chart that compares the objectives of our curricula with the objectives of the state tests. Some of you will be amazed to see how closely the objectives of our curricula correspond to those of the state tests. Likewise, the department leaders analyzed our classroom tests and assessments. They found a less clear connection between these assessments and the objectives of state tests.

The language needs to focus on the "we" and on the definition of the problem:

The entire faculty must work together to create a plan of action for the next school year that will help improve the link between our classroom tests and assessments. This plan must ensure a greater link between the objectives of the state tests and our curricula. Everyone is going to break into our problem-solving groups to begin this task. We will talk more about these groups in a few minutes.

Analyzing the Subjects and Verbs of the Principal's Message

This section discusses the principal's conscious choices of primary subjects and verbs of independent clauses for selected sentences in her presentation to the faculty. Communicators need to match sentence structure to the nature of the group in order to have the intended impact. Because the principal has taken the time to think about how to match her person to the flexibility, friendship, and professionalism of the faculty, she appreciates the significance of creating sentences that address the beliefs and attitudes of her audience.

The statements below are from parts of the principal's message. The point to remember is that her choices of sentence structure, subject, and verb are purposeful.

> (1) Our school received the data from the state tests two weeks ago. (2) The department leaders and I have reviewed the data and found a decline in student performance in most areas of reading, writing, and mathematics. (3) Student performance is our most important mission. (4) One of our responsibilities is helping our students gain the knowledge and skills they need to be successful on the state tests.

In sentence 1, the principal uses the subject *school* on purpose to establish a sense of common need among all faculty members and administration. The verb *received* indicates that the test result came from a source outside the school. It does not matter if this outside source is the central office or the testing bureau.

In sentence 2, the principal highlights the department leaders in order to show that she is not acting alone. The verb *have reviewed* demonstrates knowledge of the data. The meeting is not called as a "knee-jerk reaction."

In sentence 3, the subject *performance* creates a vision of evaluation. This choice is necessary because the principal wants to relate actions to be taken to the "student performance." The linking verb *is* equates "performance" to "mission." This connection is designed to make it clear that expected performance is necessary.

In sentence 4, the word *one* is used to communicate the idea of *this one*. There are many responsibilities, but this is the one we are going to focus on. The verb *is helping* communicates the idea of shared responsibility, even though later on the principal makes it clear that the major responsibility does lie with the teacher.

Making the Verb the Engine of Your Message / 93

Exercise

You are going to analyze the principal's choice of simple subjects and verbs for sentences 5–7. In addition, make other comments about sentence structure and other nouns.

> (5) As a faculty, we need to determine the factors contributing to our declining scores on the state tests. (6) We have successfully tackled problems with student performance before, and we can do it again. (7) Some areas to investigate could include our curricula, our tests and assessments, and our instructional strategies.

Analysis of Sentences 5–7

In sentence 5 _____
_____
_____

In sentence 6 _____
_____
_____

In sentence 7 _____
_____
_____

Further Analysis

(8) The department leaders have created a chart that compares the objectives of our curricula with the objectives of the state tests. (9) Some of you will be amazed to see how closely the objectives of our curricula correspond to those of the state tests. (10) Likewise, the department leaders analyzed our classroom tests and assessments. (11) They found a less clear connection between these assessments and the objectives of state tests.

Analysis

In sentence 8, the subject *department leaders* is used emphasize that the task at hand was determined by peers, as well as the principal. The verb *have created* illustrates that the "leaders" have actively participated in the development of the chart, rather than being handed the chart by the principal.

In sentence 9, the word *some* is purposefully used to imply that certain individuals might already understand the problem at hand. This in essence is asking participants to reflect for a moment to determine if the department leader findings really surprise them. If participants are *not* surprised, then they automatically buy into the problem and the need for a solution. The verb *will be amazed* is used to awaken those participants who have no idea what is going on.

Exercise

You are going to analyze the principal's choice of simple subjects and verbs for sentences 10 and 11. In addition, make other comments about sentence structure and other nouns.

Analysis of Sentences 10 and 11

In sentence 10 _____
_____
_____

In sentence 11 _____
_____
_____

Following Up Dr. J.'s Decision-Making Plan

Once the teachers have completed their group work during the in-service day and additional meetings, Dr. J. obviously needs to evaluate the combined products. However, she probably would create a team composed of one member from each group to assist her. The goal is that changes are not made without teacher approval. Otherwise, the exercise becomes a waste of time and the faculty would resent being duped. Dr. J. might try to ask the central office for a small amount of funds to pay the teacher representatives for a few hours of summer work in order to ensure that the final plan is logical and complete.

Immediately after the professional development meeting at the end of school, the principal sends a letter to participants thanking them for their efforts. The words chosen in this memo emphasize her appreciation. In addition, the content sets up a positive attitude toward future decision-making sessions.

Below is the first paragraph of this follow-up letter.

> (1) Your determination to create a meaningful test improvement plan will benefit our students and the quality of our instruction.

96 / Chapter 6

(2) We engaged in thoughtful and respectful conversation and problem solving. (3) Members of each group listened carefully as the department leaders explained this year's testing results. (4) As professionals, you used this data effectively in designing our school's new assessment plan. (5) Linking state test objectives to our curricula, instruction, and assessment will have a significant impact on student learning and achievement.

Analysis

In sentence 1, the subject *determination* reestablishes a feeling that the work was not easy, but staff stuck with it. The verb *will benefit* reminds the teachers of the payoff.

In sentence 2, the subject *we* again focuses on the group effort and creates a personal touch. The verb *engaged* emphasizes the idea of being actively focused.

Exercise

Analyze the principal's choice of simple subjects and verbs for sentences 3–5 above. In addition, make other comments about sentence structure and other nouns.

Analysis of Sentences 3–5

In sentence 3 _____
_____
_____

In sentence 4 _____
_____
_____

In sentence 5 _____
_____
_____

7
Organizing Your Message with the Proper Perspective

Category 3: Asking the Right Questions

Effective questioning is based on a well-thought-out appreciation for the audience and that audience's relationship with the administrator. One way to gain valuable insight into this relationship is to create a frame. A frame, much like a picture frame, presents a clear structure that focuses the message within it.

Gerry Brenner, the author of a commentary on the great Hemingway novel *The Old Man and the Sea*, uses the concept of the frame to draw conclusions about the main character's, Santiago's, behavior. Brenner employs the relationship between Santiago and Manolin, the boy whose respect Santiago seeks, as the central thread that defines the frame. Specifically, Brenner defines the framing through the conversations between Santiago and Manolin in the beginning of the book. Without this framing, the triumphant ending where Santiago brings the marlin's carcass to shore would not be as significant.

The administrator needs to create his or her frame defining the relationship between him- or herself and the individual or group who will receive the message. This definition centers on three factors.

1. **A significant event or interaction that has had an important impact on the relationship.** For example, a teacher might have received a poor evaluation from the administrator previously and has continued to feel bitter about this evaluation. Or the administrator might have appointed a science teacher as "acting department head," allowing this individual to transition into the job permanently. A teacher might also feel resentful because the administrator has failed to recognize certain achievements.
2. **Previous experiences of working together on tasks.** For example, the administrator and the teacher might have served together on a committee to appoint a new superintendent; during this experience they discussed children and family issues. Or the administrator may have asked the teacher to present information with him or her during a parent-teacher meeting, and the teacher was unprepared.
3. **The match or mismatch of approaches and attitudes.** For example, a teacher might agree with the administrator about providing more structured tasks in the classroom. Or, when the principal has proposed each teacher work with the district technical support staff to create and update a web page with assignments, comments, and messages for parents, a teacher may have been vocally opposed to the idea.

Here's the bottom line: the frame defines the relationship between the administrator and the recipient of the message. The frame does not need to address all three of the factors given above, but the principal should consider each one while developing the frame.

The following example illustrates the thinking process involved in framing. The first example only centers on factor 1. The same thinking processes need to be used with factors 2 and 3.

Case Study

Mrs. H., a school administrator, thinks Mrs. D., a fourth grade teacher, is still angry with her for not nominating her as teacher of the year last May. It is now the following October, and a new teacher of the year will not be nominated for a number of months. Mrs. D. still works hard and is a terrific teacher, but Mrs. H. knows she is unhappy. Whenever Mrs. D. is asked to work on a project, like writing the new science curriculum, she does a great job.

Mrs. H. needs to assemble a group of teachers to develop and deliver a parent program about changes in the elementary school curriculum. She knows that Mrs. D. is the perfect person to lead this group. Members of the teacher group will receive a small stipend, but they will not be adequately paid for the time it will take to design the program.

Mrs. H. has asked Mrs. D. if she could meet with her for a few minutes after school to discuss leading this group. In preparation for this meeting, the principal has spent a few minutes thinking about the frame that helps to define their relationship.

From these reflections, Mrs. H. thinks about the questions that will help her define how she is going to communicate with the teacher. Once the principal has "framed" the relationship between herself and the teacher, she generates a list of questions to consider. Some of these questions will become part of the principal's message, but others will not.

Reflection on Relationship	*Framing Questions*
She is still angry at me about the Teacher of the Year nomination.	How can I get her district recognition so she won't be angry with me? How do I start off in a positive way? Do I mention what a great job she is doing? Do I compliment her in any way? How do I praise her skills? Do I tell her now that I am going to nominate her for Teacher of the Year next May?

This list of questions is not complete, but it represents Mrs. H.'s initial thinking. The administrator can create these questions in her mind or record them. Either way, using the framing to solidify an understanding of the relationship is important. Once responses to these questions have been contemplated, the administrator can create an even more purposeful message. The process of generating these framing questions is completed very quickly after limited practice. Then the administrator will refine the actual language to be used with the recipient once the questions related to framing are considered.

The principal is already familiar with Mrs. D.'s flexibility, friendliness, and professionalism. She knows that Mrs. D. is highly flexible, friendly, and professional. This understanding means that the key issue to consider is her feelings after being overlooked for teacher of the year.

The framing questions help the principal to determine an optimum language tactic that will increase the likelihood of the teacher's participation in a leadership role. Once the principal has generated the list of framing questions, she needs to make sure that the definition of the outcome behavior is clear in her mind.

> **Outcome Behavior:** Mrs. D. will lead the teacher's group that designs a workshop explaining curricular changes to parents. The leader will organize the workshop and define the tasks for each group member. The leader will organize the actual parent presentation.

The principal also understands that the initiation of this message must use a *direct approach*. Mrs. D. "suffers no fools" and will be offended by an indirect approach.

In preparing the structure of her message to the teacher, the principal looks over the framing questions and clusters them into group when possible. For example, these three framing questions become one grouping:

- How do I praise her skills?
- Do I mention what a great job she is doing?
- How do I start off on a really positive note?

At the same time, the principal needs to make sure the message is to the point. Here is how the principal used a direct approach and responded to these three questions.

> Parents have been raising a lot of questions about changes in the language arts curriculum. At its last meeting, the PTA president brought up the need to inform parents about these changes.
> You have done a terrific job at incorporating these changes into daily instruction. No one on the staff understands these changes better than you do.
> This information session for parents has to be well organized and clear. The session needs to be run by someone who has the respect of teachers and parents.
> Your leadership in creating this session will ensure that it is a success. The assistant superintendent and I were hoping that you would be the leader of the group that will present these changes to parents.

Analysis of the Principal's Initial Message to the Teacher

The principal began the response with the word *parents* in order to create a clear filter that guides the communication away from her. The direct approach laid out the issue immediately. The principal added the comment about the PTA to provide backup data that reinforced the validity of the issue. If the message recipient accepts the issue at this point, there is a much greater likelihood that the teacher will accept the task.

The second part zeroes in on praise without heaping on too much. Too much praise might create a backlash of resentment. The teacher might think, "If I am that great, why didn't you support me for teacher of the year?" The principal has placed boundaries around these comments so that they are centered on the issue at hand.

The third part establishes the idea that anyone is not acceptable. The person running the program has to be well organized, well informed, and articulate. In addition, this person must be liked and respected by parents.

The final part starts with praise. However, the principal knows that it might take an outside endorsement to seal the deal. So she talked with the assistant superintendent, who was very happy to add his name to the final sentence.

Here's the point: The framing questions help the principal formulate a message that addresses appropriate interventions.

Thoughts about the Use of Framing Questions

The framing questions enable the principal to think about several factors that influence the message. This type of questioning works in conjunction with the analysis of flexibility, friendship, and professionalism of the message recipient. Therefore, the framing questions are *not* merely a list of brainstormed questions about the issue. In fact, framing questions are much more centered and logical. They rely on a clear understanding of and appreciation for the principal's history with the recipient.

Here are a few points to remember.

- The framing questions provide a logical guide for quick exploration of how to approach the message.
- The framing questions help the administrator evaluate how history will impact receptivity of the message.
- The framing questions assist in generating a comprehensive direct or indirect initiation to the message.
- The framing questions help the administrator anticipate recipient responses to the message.
- The framing questions enable the administrator to think more clearly about optimum subject and verbs in spoken or written statements.

In addition, the framing questions help to solidify the following:

- A clear understanding of the behaviors necessary for success

- An appreciation for the characteristics of the person
- An explanation of how language will sell the message
- An exploration of how personal history might influence acceptance of the message

Case Study to Clarify the Process

Dr. Z., the principal, and Mr. Y., a middle school science teacher, have worked well together on several projects during the last several years, including a redesign of the science curriculum. Before becoming a principal, Dr. Z. was a high school biology teacher for thirteen years and was an assistant middle school principal for three years. Mr. Y. has been teaching for twenty years and is a well-respected member of the faculty. Last year they worked on the science textbook selection committee, chaired by Dr. Z., to select new science textbooks for all of the middle school science courses.

The committee developed criteria to judge all textbooks being considered. The criteria included providing support materials to students and their parents, alignment with the state's science test, the accuracy of the content, hands-on activities, and readability of the text. Early in the study, Dr. Z. and Mr. Y. began to disagree on which texts were best. Dr. Z. tried to convince Mr. Y. to adopt his preference because of the online materials available to students and their parents. However, Mr. Y. liked another series because he thought it was more aligned to the state's science standards. When the final vote was taken, the committee selected Dr. Z.'s preference over the strong and vocal objections of Mr. Y.

Mr. Y. has worked diligently to implement the new textbooks, but he and his colleagues have become more and more concerned that the actual content of the new texts does not address sections of the state science test. At the most recent middle school science department meeting, all of the science teachers voiced their concern about this issue.

Dr. Z. listened to the group's concerns but did not enter into a discussion of the issue at the department meeting. The principal realized that specific intervention was necessary.

Dr. Z. knew that Mr. Y. was the best teacher to lead the science staff in developing supplementary materials to fill the gaps in the text so that all the state's science standards would be addressed. Prior to meeting with Mr. Y., the principal did the following:

- He thought about the flexibility, friendliness, and professionalism that defined the teacher.
- He thought about his own levels of flexibility, friendliness, and professionalism in order to determine if there could be any conflict.
- He thought about his history with Mr. Y.
- He defined the desired change.
- He determined whether to use a direct or indirect initial approach.
- He listed some framing questions to act as a guide.
- He created the message in his mind because he was going to meet with the teacher directly.
- He reflected on the way he structured his message.

Even though this seems like a long list of steps, the principal was able to accomplish this sequence in less than ten minutes. The principal knew that this preparation could make the crucial difference in whether the teacher embraced the change or not.

Second Case Study Using Framing Questions

Previously shared experiences are an important dimension in the interaction between administrator and teacher. In this example, Mrs. H., the principal, wants to ask Mr. B., a fourth grade teacher, to become a mentor coordinator. During the past three years, efforts in mentoring new teachers have not met the expectations of the principal. Appointed mentors have spent required time with the new teachers, but the quality of the interaction has been lacking. Mr. B. is the one mentor who has shined in his interactions with new teachers during this time period.

The principal has used her observations of behavior during the past three years to determine that Mr. B is the right person for the job. She realizes that he is already spending lot of time with his mentee and also devotes many hours per week helping his fourth grade students, meeting parents, and grading papers. The role of mentor coordinator would not take up much time but would require additional responsibility.

The principal knew Mr. B. is very flexible, friendly, and professional. Therefore, the request can be straightforward, with a direct approach to the start of the message.

Next, the principal made sure that she had defined what she wanted Mr. B. to do.

> **Behavioral Outcome:** Mr. B. will become the mentor coordinator. He will work with me to match mentors properly and find appropriate mentor training. He will meet with mentors once per month and work with me, if appropriate, to resolve any issues.

Then the principal generated a set of framing questions based on the understanding of the task and the teacher's levels of flexibility, friendship, and professionalism.

Reflection on Relationship	Framing Questions
This teacher is very competent at mentoring. Other teachers need to learn from his approach and strategies.	What makes him so competent? What about his approach toward mentoring will help other mentors? How have his strategies supported the development of new teachers? What will be his duties? What is the time commitment? How can I compensate this teacher?

The principal clustered the first two framing questions together. These questions helped her to formulate a direct message in her mind.

Direct Approach Initial Message

You have really helped Ms. V. [the new teacher being mentored] in her orientation to the curriculum and school procedures. I know you have spent a lot of extra time meeting with her. She has mentioned to me how patient you are. The time you have spent assisting her with instructional techniques has been invaluable. For example, I know she struggled with differentiating her math lessons, and your modeling has made a significant difference.

Analysis of Initial Message

In sentence 1, the message starts with the pronoun *you* to direct meaning totally at the teacher. The verb *helped* creates a positive nature to the message immediately; therefore, the teacher should have a relaxed inner feeling. The second sentence uses the subject and verb *I know* in order to demonstrate a recognition of effort and appreciation.

Sentence 3 starts with "She has mentioned . . ." in order to emphasize that the level of excellence shown is recognized beyond the principal. The fourth sentence has the subject *time* and the verb *has been* coupled with "invaluable." The principal purposefully uses this structure to reinforce the idea that the time Mr. B. has invested has paid a strong dividend. The final sentence is an example that demonstrates the principal's true understanding of the teacher's skills.

The principal knows to pause after delivering the initial message. She wants to give the teacher an opportunity to respond, even if the response is a simple "Thank you." The principal uses the remainder of the framing questions to help her generate the rest of the message. She breaks her comments into three main ideas; this method helps her to remember her main points.

Main Idea 1

You have always taken your responsibility as a mentor very seriously. Your strategy of using the school calendar to help the new teachers "plan backward" to be prepared for events like parent conferences and "parents' math night" provides your mentees with an organized plan that gives them support and builds their confidence.

Analysis of Main Idea 1

The *you* as subject of the first sentence directs the positive comments at the teacher. The subject of sentence 2 is *strategy* to emphasize the knowledge and appreciation of the principal. The strategy is explained in the first part of the sentence to gain additional focus. The verb *provides* is intentional because the goal is to create an image of the teacher as a provider, as a nurturer.

Main Idea 2

One strategy that works very well is how you scheduled your time with your mentees. Your plan includes assistance in key areas and opportunities for them to get help for issues that pop up. This way of planning would be beneficial to other mentors and their mentees.

Analysis of Main Idea 2

The principal emphasize this "one strategy" because this is what the teacher needs to emphasize first. The principal is showing that he understands exactly what makes Mr. B. so successful. Before mentioning the new position of mentoring coordinator, the principal uses sentence 3 as a way to praise the teacher and state that this "way of planning" is important for all mentors to use.

Main Idea 3

I would like you to be our first mentor coordinator. Would you please help me develop a simple job description for a mentor

108 / Chapter 7

coordinator, including a reasonable time commitment? In addition, I would like you to think about how the school can compensate you for doing this job.

Analysis of Main Idea 3

The subject *I* purposefully brings the message to the principal making the request. The principal could have stated, "You would be a perfect mentor coordinator"; however, given the principal has a strong relationship with the teacher, it is more effective to state, "I am asking you . . ." By asking Mr. B. to assist in the development of the job description, the principal is encouraging him to take the position. Finally, instead of telling the teacher the type of compensation, the principal is letting Mr. B. define how he feels he should be rewarded.

Exercises to Increase Understanding and Promote Discussion

Effective questioning is based on a well-thought-out appreciation for the audience and that audience's relationship with the administrator. One way to gain valuable insight into this relationship is to create a frame. A frame, much like a picture frame, presents a clear structure that focuses the message within it.

This chapter includes three factors that help the administrator determine the appropriate frame for the communication. These factors are as follows:

1. A significant event or interaction that has had an important impact on the relationship
2. Previous experiences of working together on tasks
3. The match or mismatch of approaches and attitudes

The chapter includes in-depth examples related to factors 1 and 2. Your task is to create a scenario related to factor 3. You can base your scenario on a specific situation, or you can use your experience to design a realistic example. Once you have developed this scenario, you need to complete the following:

- An explanation of the situation that leads to the communication
- An evaluation of the staff member's levels of flexibility, friendship, and professionalism
- A brief statement of your own levels of flexibility, friendship, and professionalism
- A brief assessment of whether your own levels of these three factors have had an impact of your history with this staff member
- A clear explanation of the behavioral change needed
- A decision on whether to use a direct or indirect initial approach
- A listing of framing questions
- The actual message
- An analysis of the message structure

Each component of your task is outlined on the next several pages.

Explain the situation:

_____
_____
_____
_____
_____
_____
_____
_____
_____
_____
_____

Chapter 7

Think about the staff member's level of flexibility.
___

Think about the staff member's level of friendliness.
___

Think about the staff member's level of professionalism.
___

Think about your levels of flexibility, friendliness, and professionalism.
___

How have your own levels of flexibility, friendliness, and professionalism impacted the situation?
___

Organizing Your Message with the Proper Perspective / 111

What is the behavioral outcome necessary? How does this represent a change?

_____
_____
_____
_____
_____
_____
_____

Why would you choose a direct or indirect approach in your communication?

_____
_____
_____
_____
_____
_____
_____

What are the framing questions that will help you accomplish these outcomes?

Frame	Framing Questions
_____	_____
_____	_____
_____	_____
_____	_____
	_____
	_____

Chapter 7

Frame   *Framing Questions*

_____   _____

_____   _____

_____   _____

_____   _____

                                    _____

Record the message below.

_____
_____
_____
_____
_____
_____
_____
_____
_____
_____
_____
_____
_____
_____
_____
_____
_____
_____
_____

Organizing Your Message with the Proper Perspective / 113

Analyze your message. Make sure to discuss why you chose certain subjects and verbs, and also discuss other relevant structural decisions that you made. Write a brief analysis for each sentence.

_____
_____
_____
_____
_____
_____
_____
_____
_____
_____
_____
_____
_____
_____
_____
_____
_____
_____
_____
_____

8

Deciding Which Part of Your Statement to Emphasize

Category 4: Choosing Dependent and Independent Clauses

The dependent clause is subordinate to the independent clause. This means that the prime emphasis of the message falls in the independent clause. If there is a point to be made, this point needs to be included in the independent clause most of the time. For example:

> Teacher lesson plans need to include specific rubrics that describe criteria for success.

In this sentence, the independent clause stops with the word *rubrics*. This clause could stand on its own without further modification. The dependent clause is "that describe criteria for success." This dependent clause provides additional information about the word *rubrics* and modifies it.

By using "teacher lesson plans" as the complete subject, the writer is creating a direct filter through which the rest of the statement flows. The verb *need* expresses a categorical demand that indicates importance. Alternatives to the structure above may or may not be better forms of communication, depending on the circumstances. Here is one illustration.

Case Study on Emphasis

The principal of a middle school received lesson plans that were too general, and many plans did not included rubrics. Of greatest concern to him was that during a recent faculty meeting more than half of the teachers at the school admitted they were unsure how to use rubrics.

As a result, the principal arranged an in-service that centered on defining, creating, and using rubrics. After visiting multiple classrooms, the principal was convinced that the majority of teachers were not employing the skills learned at the in-service. Therefore, he sent a memo to the teachers using a direct approach. The memo began with the following two sentences:

> Teacher lesson plans need to include specific rubrics that describe criteria for success. These rubrics must be used as part of daily instruction.

The principal purposely included the dependent clause "that describe criteria for success." The principal included this dependent clause in order to reemphasize the idea that rubrics lead to positive results related to student performance.

The principal purposely did not include a dependent clause in the second sentence because his point was stated clearly with just the independent clause. The verb *must be used* in the second sentence stresses the connection between having a rubric and actually employing one.

Finally, the principal reiterated the reasons rubrics were important in the third sentence of the memo:

> Rubrics provide students with a clear set of learning expectations that help them focus on what is important.

Again, the principal purposely placed a dependent clause in the sentence in order to clarify the reason to use rubrics. The dependent clause is "that help them focus on what is important."

Moving Forward

During the next two months, the principal did not see a marked improvement in the number of teachers who included rubrics in their lesson plans and employed them during their daily instruction. He then devoted thirty minutes of monthly teacher meetings to answering questions about the implementation of rubrics and to giving staff an opportunity to create rubrics together. The principal also instructed content leaders to devote thirty minutes of monthly department meetings to sharing rubrics and discussing how to improve them. In addition, the principal used two in-service half-days for teachers to analyze student performance using these rubrics. As a result, the principal observed a noticeable improvement in teacher understanding of the following:

- the meaning of rubrics
- how to create a rubric
- where to find existing rubrics
- how to present the rubrics to students
- how to use rubrics to evaluate student performance

However, there were still a small number of faculty members who were not serious about their use of rubrics. In subsequent meetings with each department, certain teachers consistently reported that students did not pay attention to the rubrics and that the inclusion of these rubrics in instruction seemed to be a waste of time. Overall, the students were not behaving any more responsibly about their work when the rubrics were present than they were before rubrics were distributed.

The principal knew he had two issues going on at the same time with this small group of teachers: (1) the implementation of rubrics, and (2) the successful explanation of rubrics to students.

The principal now decided that informal meetings with selected teachers would be more productive than formal written messages or an address to the entire faculty. The principal determined that there were three behavioral outcomes that required clear action in order to achieve his goal.

The principal intended to reinforce the use of rubrics with those already using them and reemphasize the requirement to use rubrics with resistant teachers. Prior to creating the meetings, he thought about the flexibility, friendliness, and professionalism of the resistant teachers as a group and as individuals. These were the principal's conclusions.

1. The members of this group are all resistant to the idea of using rubrics.
2. As a group, most of the teachers do not favor change when the change requires additional effort.
3. Two members of the group influence the other three members of the group.
4. Three members of the group are professional in that their lessons are planned, and they do care about students. In addition, these three teachers spend time communicating with parents.
5. Two of the teachers want to do the minimum amount of work possible.
6. Two of the teachers are younger and want to be accepted by the two leaders of this group.

The principal thought about these conclusions and decided to make a plotting that showed who of the five teachers matched particular conclusions.

Teacher	A	B	C	D	E
Conclusion 1	✔	✔	✔	✔	✔
Conclusion 2	✔			✔	✔
Conclusion 3	✔			✔	
Conclusion 4	✔	✔	✔		
Conclusion 5				✔	✔
Conclusion 6		✔	✔		

From this clustering, the principal realized that he should focus his intensive efforts on Teachers A, B, and C because they were more professional. If the principal could change these three teachers, then that might create pressure on the other two teachers to take rubrics seriously. Based upon the influence of Teacher A over the other two teachers, the principal decided to separate Teacher A from the other two. However, the principal knew that the effectiveness of his actions depended on involving two other teachers who have successfully implemented the rubrics.

Using a Connection to Facilitate Thinking

Oftentimes connection making happens spontaneously. Sometimes the problem solver purposely seeks a connection. The goal is to use the connection in order to clarify the underlying issue.

In this instance, the principal happened to be taking his daily vitamins and the connection to the issue with these teachers dawned on him. The principal used an analogy to arrive at the idea of pairing the two younger teachers with experienced teachers who have successfully implemented rubrics.

This is the connection that sprang up in his mind.

> When I take certain vitamins, their effectiveness is increased if I eat a small amount of food with the vitamin. The vitamin pill binds with the food and maintains a greater potency. If I pair each younger teacher with an experienced teacher who is positive about rubrics, the effectiveness of implementation should be increased.

The Principal's History with the Teachers

The principal understood that he had to consider his own history with these teachers because previous interaction will have an impact on the current situation. After a few moments of reflection, the principal arrived at these conclusions.

Teacher A, who is experienced and professional, and the principal have generally had a good relationship. He has conflicted with Teacher A over certain policy changes, but the two have remained cordial.

Teachers B and C, who are newer teachers with strong professionalism, are on very formal terms with the principal.

Teachers D and E are both resistant to change and do not display the same level of professionalism. They and the principal do not really get along well. The principal has written up both teachers on occasion because they have not complied with district mandates. These teachers seem committed to ignoring anything that creates more work; in the past, the principal has let them get away with this attitude.

The Needed Behavioral Change

Next, the principal had to determine the specific behavioral change. This component of the thinking process is essential. Here is his definition of the desired change.

> **Behavioral Outcome:** Teachers A, B, and C will implement rubrics in one discipline during a one month period. For Teachers B and C, the mentor teachers will help them create these rubrics. The mentors will assist them in how to explain the rubrics to students and how to evaluate students papers based on the rubrics. For Teacher A, the principal will use a spoken message, followed by a written message, to make the expectations clear. Teachers D and E will be given rubrics in two content areas to implement. These teachers will implement these rubrics consistently for two units of instruction. The principal will use existing rubrics of one or two teachers who have implemented the process successfully. The principal will mentor these teachers.

Direct or Indirect Message Initiation

The principal recognized that he needed to use a direct message initiation with Teachers B and C. He needed to use an indirect approach with Teacher A. The structure and wording of the messages needed to vary depending upon the conclusion that he drew earlier in the process.

The principal began the structural decision making of his message with the two new teachers. Here is the initiation that the principal came up with. He purposely made the language more formal in order to reestablish the purpose of the communication. The principal strategically placed dependent clauses in certain sentences, shown in italic here.

> The inclusion of rubrics in everyday instruction is an important goal *that is mandated by the board of education*. Most teachers in the building are incorporating rubrics for different content areas in learning experiences. These teachers use rubrics to communicate learning expectations *that are required for success*. These rubrics allow students to evaluate their own performances and teachers to evaluate assignments.
>
> You have not been using rubrics as an active part of your daily instruction. You need to do a better job in meeting this mandate of the board of education. Last month *when I requested copies of content rubrics*, you handed in only one rubric *that was limited in scope* for a science experiment.

Analysis of Direct Initiation Message

The principal used the word *inclusion* as the subject to reinforce the idea that the rubrics need to be included. The dependent clause "that is mandated by the board of education" reminds the teachers that this policy is greater than the school level. The principal could have started this first sentence with the following: "The board of education has mandated that rubrics need to be part of daily instruction." In this case the dependent and independent clauses become reversed. The principal wanted to use the idea of "inclusion of rubrics" as the filter instead of the board of education.

Sentence 2 begins with "Most teachers . . ." to get across the idea that these teachers are in the minority; in addition, the principal wants to emphasize that most teachers are using these rubrics across the curriculum.

Sentences 3 and 4 repeat a concept that has been presented previously during meetings and workshops. The dependent clause in sentence 3 is designed to highlight that the rubrics mean "success."

The first sentence of the second paragraph begins with the pronoun *you* in order to direct the message to the teachers. The verb *have not been using* is a less formal way to making it clear that the teacher is not an active participant. The next sentence states the requirement based on the problem in the prior sentence.

The first dependent clause in the final sentence reminds the teachers that the principal has been actively involved in the process. The principal could have placed the dependent clause at the end of the sentence, but the emphasis of the principal's documentation of failure to meet expectation would be softened.

The other dependent clause reminds the teachers that the rubric they used was inadequate.

Indirect Approach Initiation for Teacher A

The principal had worked with this teacher long enough to know that he was not overly flexible but was quite professional. Teacher A took his job very seriously. However, he did not want to cooperate with any new idea that he disagreed with. In the case of rubrics, Teacher A believed they were a waste of time. "I tell my kids what they need to include in assignments all the time," he had stated at a faculty meeting.

The principal knew that in order to reach this teacher he would need use an indirect approach. This meant that the principal would need to begin his conversation with the teacher by zeroing in on an idea that the teacher would accept. The principal began to think. Then he realized that Teacher A was taking administration courses toward certification. He knew he could use this as the frame for his message.

Message Frame	*Framing Questions*
Teacher A wants to be an administrator.	How should someone wanting to be an administrator behave? Why should he accept the policy of the school board? How can his cooperation be helpful to his career? How will he set an example for other teachers?

The principal used the framing questions to generate the beginning of the spoken message to Teacher A, for whom he had some level of professional respect. The principal purposely places dependent clauses in sentences in order to emphasize key points.

Analysis of the Message to Teacher A

Sentence 1: As someone wanting to become a school administrator, you need to recognize that principals have to carry out school board policy.

The introductory clause is stated purposely to create empathy for the principal's role. If the principal had not completed the thinking related to the framing, this comment could not have been included. The subject *you* places the issue at the feet of the teacher. This choice works well because of the one-to-one meeting. The principal could have chosen the word *must*; however, *need* was less dictatorial and still got the point across. The infinitive *to recognize* is included to emphasize the idea of personal awareness, particularly considering the teacher's goal of becoming an administrator. The dependent clause, "that principals have to . . . ," emphasizes the idea that if this teacher expects to be a principal, he is going to have to deal with teachers who are not carrying out policy.

Sentence 2: School board policy dictates that rubrics be used in the classroom.

This sentence restates what the teacher already knows. The word *policy* is the subject to reinforce the idea of requirement. The verb *dictates* is chosen to show that the teacher is going to be held accountable because this is the law of the district. The contrast between the "need" in the previous sentence and "dictates" in this sentence is purposeful. The principal could have made the dependent clause, "that rubrics be used . . . ," the independent clause and placed "school board policy" at the end of the sentence; however, in this case the principal is reinforcing the idea of carrying out the chain of command because this teacher might someday have to do the same thing.

Sentence 3: I am required to ensure that all teachers follow this policy.

The subject *I* brings the point of view back to the principal's job. The verb *am required* reminds the teacher that the principal has no choice but to enforce the policy. The dependent clause, beginning with "that all teachers . . . ," is a crucial modification of the idea that the principal is required to make sure policy is carried out.

Sentence 4: Can you see that your reluctance to use rubrics presents a problem?

The use of an interrogative here is to ask the listener to use reasoning skills to understand that he is part of the problem. If the teacher responds even conditionally, the principal's point becomes strengthened.

Sentence 5: Someday you will be standing where I am informing a teacher that he or she has to follow board policy.

This final sentence is designed to create a heightened empathy since the teacher wants to become an administrator. The verb *will be standing* is purposely chosen for this reason. The dependent clause, beginning with "that he or she . . ." reinforces the need to follow board rules. If the principal did not use this dependent clause, the responsibility of the principal to follow board policy would not be explicitly stated.

As a result of this preparation, the principal knew exactly how he was going to approach the meeting with Teacher A.

Meeting with Teacher A

The principal met with Teacher A, using his predetermined language in sentences one through five above as the pillars of his message. He carefully watched the teacher's body language to determine if he seemed to be taking the message seriously. At first, the teacher assumed the message was going to be a rehash of the previous interactions about rubrics. However, when he heard the statements, his posture improved and his attention became centered on the principal.

Teacher A knew that his chances of getting an administrator's position would be greatly enhanced if the principal were willing to write him a recommendation. In reality, he may not have even entertained the likelihood that the principal would help. However, the principal was offering him an opportunity. By helping to shepherd this implementation of rubrics into the school, the principal would be a positive force in the teacher's future.

Meeting with Teachers D and E

These two teachers have become resistant to change as they have moved closer to retirement. This is especially the case if the change requires additional work. The principal needed to use a direct approach with both teachers, restating board policy and providing them with the rubrics being used by other members of their department. The principal realized that he was not direct enough with these teachers during the evolution of this issue. The principal now will make it clear that the infusion of rubrics into instruction is nonnegotiable.

Exercises to Increase Understanding and Promote Discussion

For this exercise, you will be given conditions that define a situation. These conditions can be used to write sentences to be included in your message. You need to write three sentences about each set of conditions. One sentence uses the first condition as the independent clause and the second condition as the dependent clause. The second sentence reverses the sentences structures. The third sentence eliminates the dependent clause. For example:

Condition 1: Rubrics provide criteria.

Condition 2: Rubrics help meet expectations.

Sentence 1: Rubrics provide students with specific criteria that help them meet assignment expectations.

Sentence 2: Rubrics help students to meet assignment expectations that are based upon specific criteria.

Sentence 3: Rubrics provide students with specific criteria and, therefore, help them meet assignment expectations.

Condition 1: The school board is focused on policy.

Condition 2: Teachers are required to grade all tests within two school days.

Sentence 1: _____

Sentence 2: _____

Sentence 3: _____

Deciding Which Part of Your Statement to Emphasize / 127

Condition 1: Mrs. Jones deserves heartfelt thanks for her hard work.

Condition 2: Mrs. Jones spent countless hours evaluating data.

Sentence 1: _____

_____

Sentence 2: _____

_____

Sentence 3: _____

_____

Condition 1: Parents must wait in the gym.

Condition 2: Parents pick up children.

Sentence 1: _____

_____

Sentence 2: _____

_____

Sentence 3: _____

_____

128 / Chapter 8

Condition 1: Behavior during the recent fire drill was unacceptable.

Condition 2: The school will have another fire drill next week.

Sentence 1: _____

_____

Sentence 2: _____

_____

Sentence 3: _____

_____

Throughout this book, administrator issues or problems are presented. What is a similar type of problem that you have experienced? Explain the situation and the problem below.

_____
_____
_____
_____
_____

Based on your explanation above and your best recollection of the situation, think about the flexibility, friendliness, and professionalism levels of those involved with the problem.

Flexibility: _____

_____
_____

Friendliness: _____

_____
_____

Deciding Which Part of Your Statement to Emphasize / 129

Professionalism: _____
_____
_____

Comment on your history with the staff member(s) involved.
_____
_____
_____

Would you plan to use a direct or an indirect approach to communication? Why?
_____
_____

Think about how you are going to frame the beginning of your response. Then list a few questions that will help you to structure this part of the message.

Frame	*Framing Questions*
_____	_____
_____	_____
_____	_____
_____	_____
	_____
	_____

130 / Chapter 8

Based on your reflections, develop the first part of your spoken and written message to the appropriate members of the staff. At least two sentences from each need to contain dependent clauses.

Spoken: _____
_____
_____
_____
_____
_____

On the lines below, analyze why you chose the subjects and verbs you did. Also, discuss why you placed the dependent clauses where you did.
_____
_____
_____
_____
_____
_____
_____

Written: _____
_____
_____
_____
_____
_____
_____
_____

Deciding Which Part of Your Statement to Emphasize / 131

On the lines below, analyze why you chose the subjects and verbs you did. Also, discuss why you placed the dependent clauses where you did.

_____
_____
_____
_____
_____
_____

Bibliography

Brenner, Gerry. *The Old Man and the Sea: Story of a Common Man.* New York: Twayne, 1991.

Gordon, William J. J., and Poze, T. *The Metaphorical Way of Learning and Knowing.* Cambridge, MA: Porpoise Books, 1973.

Harvey, O. J., David E. Hunt, and Harold M. Schroder. *Conceptual Systems and Personality Organization.* New York: Wiley, 1961.

Hunt, David E., and Edmund V. Sullivan. *Between Psychology and Education.* New York: Dryden Press, 1974.

Lewin, Kurt. *Principles of Topological Psychology.* New York: McGraw-Hill, 1936.

About the Authors

Robert Pauker has trained teachers and administrators, for thirty years, to implement strategies that accelerate learning. He has trained corporate and government personnel and school administrators in his methods for better report writing and critical thinking. His Structured Writing Program is designed to increase test scores. Bob is the author of several articles and books, including *Teaching Thinking and Reasoning Skills: Problems and Solutions*, published by the American Association of School Administrators.

K. Michael Hibbard earned his PhD from Cornell University, taught science, and served as a school- and district-level administrator for thirty-seven years. He is currently the assistant superintendent for instruction and human resources in the North Salem Central School District, North Salem, New York. Mike has published and consulted widely in the United States and abroad on performance assessment and is currently innovating twenty-first-century problem-solving strategies that link the classroom with the community.

www.ingramcontent.com/pod-product-compliance
Lightning Source LLC
Chambersburg PA
CBHW030115010526
44116CB00005B/265